A Gray Faith

Walking Through the Dark Parts of This Life

Bailey B. Heard

ANDREW B. HEARD

He is real!

Thank You!

Bailey B. Howard
He is real!

What People Are Saying About This Book

Few communicators write with as much passion, authenticity, and transparency as Andrew Heard. In his book, *A Gray Faith*, Andrew raises the private, public, and personal doubts and questions of those of us struggling to follow the life and teachings of Jesus of Nazareth. Andrew's Jesus-shaped life, ministry, and journey connect with the larger story of redemption in ways that may surprise you. His story shatters the neatness of faith, brings help to the hurting, strength for today, and bright hope for tomorrow. I have known him as a timely resource to a father encouraging three young men to live a Jesus-shaped life. Andrew's influence and courageous leadership in *A Gray Faith* will shine hope into your life.

—Dr. Albert Reyes, *President and CEO, Buckner International*

Whether you have found faith to be a rather easy journey or a Herculean struggle, you will find Andrew B. Heard's *A Gray Faith* to be a gripping, gut-wrenching read. Not for those in search of a "sweet story" or "easy answers," this always-honest, frequently-disquieting, richly-illustrated, and sometimes-humorous work is an autobiographical chronicling of a gifted, if haunted, young minister's quest to find peace and purpose in life and in death. Written in Faulknerian-style with a Twainian-touch, *A Grey Faith* is a courageous book offered by a persevering pilgrim, proud husband and father, and would-be cancer survivor as a defiant act of faith, love, and hope. It is a volume, one gathers, with which Mother Teresa would have readily identified and deeply resonated. Read it! Reflect upon it! Be consoled and disturbed by it! Having done so, you will be compelled to pray, "Thy kingdom come," to say, "Lord, I believe. Help my unbelief," and to cry, "Abba!" with sighs too deep for words.

—Todd D. Still, *William M. Hinson Professor of Christian Scriptures, Baylor University, Truett Seminary*

In *A Gray Faith*, Andrew bravely opens his heart to share his faith struggles and divine questions about pain and suffering. In this must read book, you will find great encouragement for anyone who has ever faced uncertainty in their faith walk or those who have questioned God. Here on earth we all see dimly but one day we shall see Him face to face and all will be clear.

—Mike Buster, *Executive Pastor, Prestonwood Baptist Church*

A Gray Faith

Walking Through the Dark Parts of This Life

ANDREW B. HEARD

Carpenter's Son Publishing

A Gray Faith: Walking Through the Dark Parts of This Life

©2013 by Andrew B. Heard

Published by Carpenter's Son Publishing, Franklin, Tennessee

Published in association with Larry Carpenter of Christian Book Services, LLC
www.christianbookservices.com

Cover Design by Debbie Manning Sheppard

Interior Design by Suzanne Lawing

Editing by Dirk Wierenga

Proofread by Andrew Toy

Printed in the United States of America

978-0-9883962-8-9

This book is dedicated to all who struggle! You are not alone, you are not wrong!

The writing of this book had to happen quickly. Writing a book while fighting for your life is not easy! I have to thank the wonderful team at Carpenter's Son Publishing. Without their help this project wouldn't have been completed.

I also need to thank my family. I have to thank my beautiful wife for her support and encouragement even when I was a monster from my Chemotherapy. My sweet daughter brought so many tears and inspiration from her wonderful spirit. My sister, father, and mother brought stability, encouragement, and ideas that I couldn't have managed without.

This book is a piece of me, but it is also comprised of the Holy Spirit and the Church as the community of believers. It was this piece that helped me break through to God when gray seemed to turn to black.

Thank You All! I love you!

Table of Contents

Chapter 1 - The Reality of Doubt 21

Chapter 2 - Doubting Ourselves 25

Chapter 3 - Doubting the Church 37

Chapter 4 - Doubting Who Goes to Heaven 45

Chapter 5 - Depression and Hope 53

Chapter 6 - The Death of Dreams 63

Chapter 7 What if? 73

Chapter 8 - Does Jesus Change People? 79

Chapter 9 - The Dirty Kid 87

Chapter 10 – What is God's Will? 95

Chapter 11 – Why I Still Believe 101

Chapter 12 – Walking in Uncertainty 111

Chapter 13 – Locked In 117

Chapter 14 – Finding God 125

Chapter 15 – God Sweeps In 131

Foreword

In his song *Honesty*, Billy Joel wrote, "Honesty is such a lonely word. Everyone is so untrue. Honesty is hardly ever heard. And mostly what I need from you." I may not be as cynical as Billy Joel but I think he's right. One of the most uncommon of all human qualities is honesty. From our hurried personal encounters with one another resulting in very few meaningful conversations, to our happy lives posted on Face Book and Instagram, it's rare to get the truth and nothing but the truth. Honesty is a precious gift. That's why I love Andrew so much. I'm at once challenged and liberated every time I'm with him. I'm challenged to be more honest with myself and my faith and I'm set free to be myself. Andrew is one of the most courageous people I've ever known. And it's not because of his athletic accomplishments or his overcoming stage four Hodgkin's lymphoma right out of high school, or even that he is currently battling an aggressive cancer that just might take his life. Andrew is brave because he's honest.

I am convinced that it is the few who choose to be truly honest- with God, with themselves, and with others- these are the ones who reach their fullest redemptive potential. This is courage: to name your struggles, declare your doubts, let others in, and with everything you've got, wrestle it all to the ground. I'm so grateful that Andrew has allowed me, and now all of us, into his story.

This book is a great gift, not only to those who claim to believe, but to anyone who wants to approach faith with intellectual integrity. Andrew has a brilliant mind and has thought more deeply about his faith than most people even have the capacity to do. As an apologist, I've come to agree with Andrew that *gray faith* is really the only kind of faith. Oh, the black and white will come, but not on this side of eternity. Faith always precedes reason on this side. It's why Paul said, "For now we see only a reflection as in a mirror; then we shall see face to face. Now I know in part; then I shall know fully, even as I am fully known" (1 Corinthians 13:12). Andrew has learned how to live in the glorious tension of the "already" and "not yet" reality of the Gospel. Andrew teaches us to bring faith and reason together into a life filled with hope. In Romans 8:24, Paul says, "For in this hope we were saved. But hope that is seen is no hope at all. Who hopes for what they already have?" I've watched the power of hope come alive in Andrew. I've seen a transformation in his life that can only be explained by the very presence of God.

In the pages ahead, Andrew is courageous and trusting enough to let us in on some of the deepest struggles of his faith journey. I had conversations with Andrew during some of the darkest nights of his soul. If you've ever come to the end of your faith, when you were ready to bail on Jesus altogether, be assured, Andrew has been there. We've talked about the fact that his journey is not unlike Job's. Job had to decide whether he worshipped God because of all that He had done for him or if he would worship God simply because He's God. And how would Job ever know? There's really only one way: Strip Job of everything God had given him; then he would know. This is Andrew's journey. And it's why he can now write a book like this. Through his horrific battle with cancer and even more, his fierce battle of faith, Andrew's response echoes Job's. "My ears had heard of you but now my eyes have seen you" (Job 42:5). In the end, Job didn't get all of his answers. He got something better. He got *God*. This is the story Andrew wants to tell. He got God. And once you truly get ahold of God, not only do you not need your answers, you don't need anything else. Even better, you've got nothing to lose. And that's where a life of courage begins. Thank you Andrew for this amazing book and even more, for the gift of your amazing life to us all.

Dr. Jeff Warren
Park Cities Baptist Church, Dallas, Texas

Introduction

Standing there, I could feel my chest tightening. Though I was surrounded by people who seemed so happy, all I could feel was confusion and pain. The band was playing, the lights were low, but my heart was hurting.

I looked over to my friends and none of them had any idea what I was feeling. How could they know? There was no way I was going to tell them. I couldn't. I was in seminary for goodness sake! Seminary students didn't have these feelings. Looking up toward the balcony, the circular sanctuary of Highland Baptist Church in Waco, Texas was filled with college students.

I had been attending the church for a few months, though I hadn't really become a part of the group. As a seminary student it was hard to get plugged in. Everyone seemed to look at us seminary types a little strange - as if a twenty year old seminary student was some kind of freak. While others are trying to avoid parties, seminary students are struggling with the teachings of some two thousand year old dead guy through books that librarians don't seem to care about.

Here I was attending a seemingly joyous worship service for college students and I wanted to cry. When I tried to sing, my mouth opened but no words came out. Even though I wanted to be just as happy as those around me, instead I was hurting and didn't understand why. For the first time I struggled to understand. All my life I had tried to do what was right, but struggling to believe was something new.

As the song ended, my anxiety began to drop a bit. Even though I knew they wouldn't, I still wished they would cut the service short. As a preacher myself, I knew they wouldn't announce, "Well, we're done with singing today." That wasn't going to happen, but I hoped desperately that it would. I couldn't listen to another sermon where the biggest objections to my faith were ignored even though the people around me were saying "yes." But yes to what?

The preacher's name was Kyle and he was a good man. As he started, I felt myself cave in, and to this day have no idea what he said. It could have been the most miraculous sermon, but the battle raging in my soul was too loud to hear it.

The words of the preacher bounced off of me like water off a rock. Flooded with emotion, I stood up and walked out of the sanctuary. It was the first time I'd ever walked out a service because of unbelief. As I left, there was a feeling of guilt slamming into my chest in a torrent of emotion. Tears welled up in my eyes as I walked over to the nearest chair.

My soul was crushed. I hadn't come to this place easily, having grown up in church and for most of my life being filled with confidence that my faith was true. Though I had sometimes experienced small doubt, it was nothing that felt as if it would overwhelm me. Most of my security came from the fact that I could logically think through my belief system and understand what my faith was all about.

I have always been a prideful person and have fought the tendency to be self-absorbed. When I was younger, the fight wasn't as strong and I'd fight less effectively against self-centeredness—more like a cuddling match. As a child, you realize that you should think about others, but it doesn't seem that important. It doesn't seem that important that your friends get to score as much as you do in the game, or that you respond with grace when people complement you. I really had a hard time with complements when I was young. I liked it when people said nice things, but it made me feel awkward. I hadn't realized that their compliment could be absorbed and be just about me or deflected and absorbed. Deflected and absorbed meant that I thanked the person and passed along the achievement to all those involved; instead, I just looked at them an acted as if it was perfectly natural that I receive such praise. I didn't mean to be a jerk, but I succeeded at it quite well. [This whole part about absorbed and deflected and absorbed doesn't make any sense.]

One event changed my tendency toward inward focus. At eighteen I was struck with stage four cancer. One might think that facing death would have made me less focused on myself. But the truth is, it can make one even more focused on themselves. For a while I was consumed with my own mortality. It wasn't until I started to recover that my focus began to shift. Though it was a slow shift, thankfully over the course of three to four years, God worked mightily in my life.

The change started while I was still sick. I went in for a checkup at M.D. Anderson in Houston where I found my condition was improving. My cancer was in retreat and I was feeling fairly healthy. The hospital was busy that day resulting in me being pushed into a waiting room with some of the patients from the pediatric ward. It was the first time I had ever been in a room with kids sick with cancer.

The reality of those hurting children stabbed deep into my soul. For the first time, I started to see other people in the hospital. It wasn't that I hadn't seen them before; it was that I hadn't cared. That was the first time I felt overwhelmed with sympathy for my fellow terminals.

A small eight year old boy who was crying caught my attention. He had a cup of barium in one hand and a needle sticking in his other arm. Just looking at that cup made me want to vomit from the memory of my own treatment and I knew the needle burned because the one that was in my own arm had been burning for an hour.

I still feel the tears start to flow thinking about that little boy. I don't know if he lived or died, nor do I know his name. But I will never forget him. As I looked at him that day for the first time, I questioned whether I could trust God. Why was God allowing this little boy to suffer this way? What had he done that was so evil? He wasn't even old enough to know what real evil was!

It was at that moment that I started to see the world from the perspective of other people. Prior to that, I had never really stopped to consider others nor had I walked the world from inside someone else's shoes. I had definitely not considered what the world was like for someone born in a non-Christian home.

God refined me in college. He stripped me of my sin and brought me closer to him. He mostly did this through people. God put people in my life that challenged me, and he removed me from relationships that hindered me. Being refined this way is difficult to go through because many young people don't realize the pain they inflict on others when they enter into and leave relationships. Relationships are some of the most sacred things in this life and should be treated with care. Even when we need distance from someone, we should pursue that distance with grace and concern for the other person. I failed at this tremendously in college, but I did run from my sin. In running from my sin, I may have committed further sin and all I can do now is ask for forgiveness. After college came seminary, and seminary during that time brought me to the chair outside that sanctuary. It opened me up to people and thoughts that were larger than me.

We had just finished studying Arius who was at the center of the controversy of the Council of Nicaea. For those who haven't seen the movie *The Da Vinci Code*, the Council of Nicaea took place in 325 A.D. and was where the church determined for the first time that Jesus was, in fact, God. Arius, an important figure in the early church, wrote a treatise that caused the church to rally to a council. In his treatise, Arius argued that Jesus wasn't God. His basic argument was similar to what Jehovah's Witnesses now believe. My problem was that I couldn't reason past the case presented by Arius. This was due to him being one of the fathers of our faith. Had he been someone who randomly came to my door to present an argument, I would not have been affected in the same way. But Arius was a well respected early theologian whose belief differed from mine.

Mentally, Arius broke me and I was in a struggle that I couldn't win. The anxiety that came with not having certainty about who my God was felt like an anvil on my chest. But that wasn't all that weighed on me.

Prior to this, my mind was already starting to attack my heart (or maybe it was my heart attacking my mind). After seeing that little boy in the hospital, I started to think about other people in the world - those who didn't grow up with the Gospel close to their heart.

I believe with all my heart the words of John 14:6 where Jesus says, "I am the way and the truth and the life. No one comes to the Father except through me." I believe Jesus is the only way to redemption and is our only salvation. But what does it mean for the child dying of cancer in India who has never heard the Gospel?

That was the thought that caused me to leave worship at Highland Baptist Church that night. If God is a good and loving God who loves the whole world, then why has he let the world continue on its devastating course? If the road to salvation is that narrow, why did he create us in the first place? The thought that billions of people go to hell and only a few are saved was tearing me to pieces.

Though I wanted to include more people in salvation, how could I? Where did Scripture point to more people being saved than those who hear the name of Jesus? There was no intellectual support for what my heart longed to believe. To me, the Scriptures seemed convoluted. On one hand, the Scriptures said that God was loving and desired all to be saved, but on the other hand, he seemed to be limited.

God brought salvation to the world through Jesus in Israel. But what about the people living in Korea at the time of Jesus' death? They didn't get the chance to hear Jesus' teachings before they died. What about the Native Americans? The story of Jesus wouldn't reach them for another 1500 years. Did God love them? How could he create them and know that their only hope of redemption would never reach their ears?

And let's not forget the millions of people who lived *before* Jesus! How did God love them? In Scriptures class at seminary, we talked about the ban. The ban was the time in Israel's history when God told them to destroy every human living in Palestine after they came out of Egypt. How does Scripture show God's desire for these people to be saved? My professors told me that the nation of Israel was missional. But how was it missional to destroy children in Palestine? Where is the mission to save those children and their parents? If God loved all men and desired them to come to a saving knowledge of him, where do the people destroyed in the ban fit in?

Those questions plagued my mind as I cried outside the sanctuary that night in Waco. I didn't know how I could love God when I didn't understand him. It broke my heart that he felt so distant from me. I struggled with God for so long and I felt that the battle was lost. I wanted to give up, but knew I couldn't.

That night I didn't give up, at least not completely. Instead, I numbed myself to the thoughts that wretched my gut. At first I sought help from my professors. But as hard as they tried, their answers didn't fix the problems I was having with God. To stop the pain, I stopped reading the Old Testament because I couldn't handle it. Much like Martin Luther, I felt a God I didn't understand. Instead, I focused in on a very narrow aspect of God and I put on blinders to everything else.

While I don't recommend going through life wearing blinders, it is important to know that when you don't look around, you break things, knock things over, and, in general, fail to live the life you are meant to live. Though I don't recommend walking through life with blinders, there are times when focusing and keeping your head down are the only things that keep us alive.

Slowly, as the carnage that seminary left in my soul healed, God again opened my eyes to the questions that plague our world. The questions I asked that night at church aren't left only for me to ponder, they are questions that we all ask.

If you are asking questions today, if you are crying and scared to look up as I was, I want you to know that it's okay. God expects us to ask questions. It is also okay to feel scared. God is big enough for your questions and he is strong enough to deal with your fear. While some may feel they are betraying God by doubting, I also felt the same way. Some people doubt God for a long time.

God is not caught off guard by human betrayal, nor does it do any good to lie to him about how you feel. Do you think he can be tricked by our lame excuses to cover our doubt? He already knows and he doesn't want you to run from it. Instead he wants you to embrace him more deeply while searching him out more thoroughly.

When you do search him out, it is interesting how he will answer your questions (though I know that many believers think God only answers questions through the book of Ecclesiastes). Many people think God only speaks through ancient cryptic texts and that you have to be a theologian or pastor to navigate the waters of Scripture and divine truth. Instead, there is great merit in laypeople seeking explanation of God's Word. After all, he uses his Word to instruct us and it holds all the revelation we need to know our God. However, Yahweh will meet you where you are.

I wish to tell you how this book started. From the paragraphs above, you may think that this was some supernatural moment of theological reflection that sparked my desire to wade through the deep regions of salvific history. Let me assure you, that wasn't the case. I was simply trying to be relevant to high school students.

I once did a series of messages based on Romans after taking a job as a high school minister in Dallas. I'm convinced only I would ever think that dealing with the book of Romans would be a good way to connect to a group of a few hundred teenagers.

I started writing this book after all the questions of faith flooded back into my life. I hadn't yet finished writing it as new questions pushed my faith into a new realm. I ventured in that direction to complete it. My questions led to me leaving the church and into a depression. That, combined with the fact that someone so consumed with these questions was trying to lead a youth ministry where the speed in which someone could eat a Twinkie was of paramount importance.

The reason I took this book back on is because after only a few months after leaving the ministry I was diagnosed with stage four lung cancer which has a prognosis of eight months to live.

I invite you to walk through this with me in order to explore some of the most difficult questions about God. Before starting this journey, know that I will not answer your questions. It is my hope that God may make things a little clearer for both of us. I am not in the business of answering questions. Not answering questions has been one of the hardest conclusions for me to learn.

I have always been a man who likes answers. But lately I don't find answers or bring people to conclusions in the way I once thought I had. The purpose of my journey is not to find the answer. Instead, I am on a journey with the Answer.

Let's stroll together and hope we find that our walk takes us through the gray mist where we once stood toward a new ground with new questions. "May we find that in the mist, we see the cross, and through the cross, we see our world."

CHAPTER 1

The Reality of Doubt

Doubt, as experienced in the abstract, is something that is easily ignored. I find that Christians continually speak of trusting God in Sunday school. However, the problem with talking about trusting God in a church setting is that it has no value unless the uncertainty of the world is brought into the room. This is because only when the distance of tragedy is shortened to the touch of a finger that the true test of faith takes place.

For most of my life I have felt a great enough distance from people that I was numb to the pain of losing someone. In more recent times, I have encountered people whom I care about that have experienced great pain. It is in the midst of their pain that doubt threatens to overwhelm me.

The greatest pain is to watch my wife and child cry. Recently I walked into a room where I found my wife crying as she held our little girl. Though Ellie is too little to understand why Mommy was upset, she became emotional because her mom was upset. I witnessed this when I walked into the back room of my parent's house. It was enough to rip my heart from my chest.

Bailey sat rocking Ellie with tears streaming down her face. My wife has a beautiful face with creamy white skin that turns red when she is upset. Her lower lip quivered and she started to wail. I walked over and wrapped my arms around her but didn't know what to say. What does one say when confronted by such sorrow?

I had just come home from the doctor's office where I heard my dad's voice while sitting in the examination room. This was not a good sign. Though it was my dad's office, I always saw one of the other physicians when I went to the clinic. From outside the examination room I could hear Dad say, "I'll tell him." Those weren't the words that I wanted to hear. The door opened and all six feet, two inches of my father walked through the door. Distress was spread across his face.

With a choked voice, he told me my tumor was back. As the words came out, everything seemed to slow down for a moment. It is one thing to think you might be sick, it is quite another to hear someone say it out loud. Upon hearing the news, I crossed the room to my dad and hugged him deep and hard. He cried as he said he was sorry. At that moment I hugged him harder and said I loved him.

In one afternoon, my world had changed. I went from a healthy twenty-nine year old husband and father, to a stage four lung cancer patient. There was a five centimeter tumor in my left lung with metastasis in my right shoulder bone and left leg. Do you know what the median survival rate of people with my cancer is? Eight months.

After hugging my father, I went home and sat in the driveway for a long time. I had cancer ten years before and it was stage four, but I didn't have a wife and daughter then. I was sitting in my car because I had no idea how to tell my twenty-seven year old wife, who was holding my toddler, that I had stage four lung cancer. How do you start that conversation?

I want to know why I, or anyone else, has to have that conversation. Why does God let five year old girls get incurable cancer? Recently I sat down with a grandmother who told me about her granddaughter who has a rare irredeemable cancer. She was amazingly positive and said it had to do with the fact that the little girl handled the situation so well. She told me that her granddaughter was as feisty as they come. To illustrate the point, she told me a story about how her granddaughter had to wear a wig and while at a birthday party some little boy pulled it off her head and laughed at her. The little girl came over to her grandparents and asked them to fix her wig and then asked if she could pull the little boys hair out. (Though the grandmother told her no, I would have said "heck, yes!" and agreed to her pulling his hair.) Stories about the innocence of children have always been an inspiration to me. However, their stories also make me question God. I want to know why there are so many children in Third World countries who are dying of disease. I also want to know why children all over the world are abused. As a child my mother-in-law was abused by her stepfather and later by her foster parents. To this day, my wife cries when she thinks about her mom growing up. That's not fair! Nor is it fair that she may also have to deal with me dying one day.

I have doubts whether God will heal me. Some might say that I don't have faith. Studying Scripture, God hasn't promised me that he will heal me from cancer. As a result, I can't have faith in a promise that isn't there. The more important question is how to have faith when my doctor says that on average I have eight months to live. Do I pray that I will live longer? Each day thousands of people find themselves in my situation and pray for healing. However, God doesn't heal all of them. Does that mean God isn't real or that he doesn't care?

Over the ages, many people have had similar questions for God. If you are one of them, read on, this is the book for you. There is no bull in this book, it is just honesty from a dying Christian.

Walk with me through what may possibly be my last days. Let's walk together with God because maybe it will bring strength to our doubt. I think we have the right to doubt God on some things. But the question is, what things? How we think about this question is most important to me.

My doubts about God not healing me and my response will determine how I live the last days of my life. Viewing my life may also determine how you live out the final days of your life. We can only hide from the reality of doubt if we refuse to engage the world. There is so much pain on this planet, thus having doubt is to be expected. But does having doubt mean we have a smaller faith? Are we bad Christians for doubting? Does questioning our beliefs mean that we're essentially questioning God's existence?

I don't know if my daughter will ever have an actual conversation with her father. She may not have her dad to walk her down the isle. These are just a few of my doubts that I plan on sharing. For centuries the Christian church has tried to make things sterile in a world that is not neat nor packaged cleanly. The Gospel is both dirty and powerful, scary and revolutionary.

It is time for us to get dirty (and scared) in the hope that it revolutionizes our lives.

CHAPTER 2

Doubting Ourselves

After six days of throwing up, I was fairly sure that I was in the sixth circle of hell.

Feeling sick to my stomach is demoralizing. On one hand you know that you need food, but nothing stays down. Then after it comes back up, you never want to touch food again.

I cried a lot this week and, for a few days, was mean as a viper. Not being able to play with my daughter was like having the family jewels sent to watch the Nutcracker. We were supposed to celebrate our five year wedding anniversary but instead I was mean and puked in front of my wife three times with the worst concoction of vomit I have ever seen.

Multiple nights I talked to my dad about what an ass I've been, and cried because I was scared. A week is a long time to feel sick. Psycho-logically, it messes with you. In my list of top ten bad weeks, this was pretty high up there. At one point I didn't know if I had the strength to make it. (I'm still not sure I have the strength to make it.)

All the pain of this week has brought a lot of clarity to my life. One might think that I was worried most about whether or not I would go to heaven. Yes, I have thought about death. My treatment this week was much harder on me than my last stage four cancer treatment. However, what I cried and worried most over was my inability to make the lives of my wife and child better. It made me feel out of control realizing that there is little I can do while undergoing treatment.

Both times after my first week of treatment after stage four cancer diagnosis, I have come away with the same truth: Don't live your life scared of death. God is the only one who can take care of that. Instead, live your life pushing death out of other people's lives.

For everyone, pushing out hell looks different. You will know it when you feel it. Bringing the Kingdom of God into someone's life means encouraging them to be all they can be. It means forgiveness and grace, hugs and songs, compassion and accountability. It is where the meek feel strong and the poor feel rich.

The question is, Why is there so much hell to push out of this world? This is the question I asked in the previous chapter. However, if we are going to doubt God, we must also ask if we should doubt ourselves. When we think of ourselves we usually think in black and white plus caveats. We say things like, "I'm a good man, but I have a little anger problem." Sometimes we make the caveat a temporal suspension of who we are: "I was a bad guy, but then I got married." In this chapter I want you to drop the black and white picture of yourself and instead examine yourself in full color. If we are going to treat God this way, it is impor-tant that we look at ourselves through the same lens.

I have recently come upon one of the most refining times in my life. Though I have only been married for only two years, I have found out more about myself in that short time than the preceding twenty-four years. What I have found (which I know will not come as a shock to my mother) is that I have a ridiculous need to be right.

I feel I'm right all the time. It makes sense that I think that way because if I thought I was wrong, I wouldn't be thinking it. While things always make sense in my head, the truth and what's in my head aren't always the same thing.

My desire to be right didn't start with my marriage. It seems from the time I was born I felt the need to pass blame. The writer of Genesis spells out this truth perfectly, telling how Adam blamed Eve for tricking him into eating the fruit. Our desire to justify is as old as time; it starts at such a young age.

When I was about ten I had an experience that I'll never forget. At the time, the response to my evil was justification. There comes a time in most young men's lives when they are introduced to the projectile. I am not sure what it is about throwing or shooting things, but boys are fascinated by them. Perhaps our obsession with launching objects into the air comes from the times when our ability to throw rocks or arrows determined our ability to provide for our families.

Despite not understanding the reason for our fascination with projectiles, that fascination grabbed me at age ten. I had two friends that came over to hang out at my house on a regular basis, and one day they brought along a sling shot. As I shot that sling shot, I remember how awesome I thought it was. We would set up cans and other targets in the yard and I was able to knock them over while standing all the way on the other end. It was amazing. I felt like I was Prometheus and had just stolen a new fire from the gods.

The problem soon became that, just like every titan who steals from the gods, I had consequences coming. It wasn't long before shooting cans and other objects seemed dull. We had learned this great ability and now we felt like we were wasting time shooting those silly cans. It was soon time to put our skills to a real test.

I am not sure how young boys come up with the lame ideas that draw them into such trouble, but there is no doubt that they have an uncanny ability to attract trouble. We soon attracted trouble alright. Trouble for us came in the form of my very angry middle-aged neighbor. It wasn't until he broke through our front door screaming that I knew we had taken it too far and that I was going to have to devise a way to pass the buck.

My neighbor's anger was legitimate. To the disgust of the now twenty-nine year old version of me, we decided that our new target should be ... well, him, standing out in his yard talking to his mom. And our choice of artilary was not feathers or cotton balls, but rocks, half the size of my fist. I still have no idea what we were thinking. It was stupid and mean, and there was no way we were going to get away with it. When the consequences came down on me, I did what so many others do: I ran to the back of the house and hid in the hamper with the dirty clothes.

Yeah, I was a real titan. My new-found sanctuary brought me just enough courage to hide as my neighbor screamed for my head. You can imagine what happened next. Realizing how terribly wrong I had been to shoot rocks at my neighbor, I crawled out of the hamper, expressed deepest sorrows for my actions and asked for forgiveness.

Actually, only part of that last line was true. While I did crawl out of the hamper, I didn't admit my guilt. My mom took the brunt of the man's anger. After he was gone, she laid into me. Being the brave young man that I was, I immediately blamed the whole thing on my friends. I mean, it was their sling shot, right? They were the ones that introduced me to my new addiction of shooting stuff and had tempted me to do wrong.

Looking back, I see much of Adam's temptation in me. If my neighbor ever reads this, I want him to know I am sorry. The problem is, while I don't shoot people with rocks anymore (realizing nowadays they would throw me in jail if I ran through the streets of Dallas sling shot happy), there is still a part of me that still longs to pass the blame. As a result, the more I think of myself as right, the less I see of God.

What if we realized there was more wrong with us than right? What if we are not the superhero in our story. What if we accepted the fact that we are actually the villains? There is a scene in the popular Twilight book series that begs us to ask a question. In this scene Bella, the human love interest, is talking with Edward, the vampire love interest, and there is one question on the table. What is Edward? Bella has seen things in him that she can't explain. He is stronger and faster than he should be. She has discovered that Edward isn't like everyone else. However, she doesn't know why.

Edward asks Bella to guess how he is different. As she begins talking about radioactive spiders and kryptonite, Edward realizes what she is saying. Bella is alluding to superheroes. He laughs at her and tells her she isn't even close. This makes Bella angry. She tells him that she will figure it out eventually. This makes Edward's tone change.

He looks at Bella and says, "I wish you wouldn't try." Bella is confused but continues to pursue an answer. Edward's response is illuminating.

"What if I'm not a superhero? What if I'm the bad guy?"

How many of us would be willing to say what Edward said? It is our inability to see this very basic truth about ourselves that keeps us in the dark and prevents us from growing.

Examples of human evil are shown on television news all the time. One example is when Major Nidal Malik Hasan unleashed his fiery hell on the Fort Hood army base on November 5, 2009. On that day Hasan, a military psychiatrist, brought a loaded weapon into a large military gathering and opened fire. During the senseless attack Hasan killed thirteen people resulting in the families of his victims losing fathers, mothers, brothers, sisters, sons and daughters. All because of the evil hidden in one man's heart.

I don't know what caused Hasan to walk onto the military base that day and begin shooting. The media has tried to place the blame on a number of different things. Some have said that it was an Islamist attack on the American military. Others have claimed that Hasan just cracked under the pressure of knowing he was about to be deployed.

While I don't know what triggered Hasan's actions, I do know why he did it. He did it because at the heart of unredeemed humanity is evil. Normal people don't simply respond to stimuli in our world. There are thousands of people who have felt the pressure of being deployed and thousands more that disagree with the American involvement in the Middle East. The vast majority of those who serve never commit murder. Instead, Hasan had a decision to make and he decided to let the darkness win.

Without Jesus, darkness always wins. Our darkness may not look like Hasan's, but it is no less real. Do you know of people in whom you harbor hate? Often sin sneaks out when no one can hear it or see it. Are you impatient with your family? Since there is no denying who you really are, what can you do to change? Can you simply choose to do right? If you have tried to be perfect for very long, I ask, How is that going for you? It's either not going well or it's about to. We're not perfect. What can we do to remove the evil that sits at our doorstep?

The evil in us must be addressed. How then, will God deal with us? How will he deal with those who are evil at the core? Events in our daily lives testify to the fact that we often choose darkness.

I don't know how that makes you feel, but it crushes me. If I say that I am behaving well and deserving good things, it only takes a short time for my actions to prove me wrong. Often I have to ask how God could love me. If you think that you're an easy person to love, you probably aren't examining your actions, motives, or thoughts very well. Take some time today to really look at your day. Have you been jealous of anyone? How about angry or impatient? Have you felt anxious? Take a moment and examine your life for imperfections. The more you look, and the more you become accustomed to what imperfection looks like, the more imperfections you will find. The imperfections we find are symptoms of something greater.

People often ask, "Why does God punishes us?" If that is the way I was born, why does God have a problem with it? It is because he loves us. He can't stand to see us to become evil nor taken down a path that leads away from him. It is not because he is jealous for our attention, it is because he knows what will happen if we move away from him. He knows what we will become and doesn't want to see it happen. Evil brings out God's wrath because it causes harm to the ones he loves.

What happens to us as God's wrath is revealed against evil? If we are the agents of evil in our world, and are evil at the core, what will God do with us? Paul sees the answer to this question in Jesus who dealt with evil. Jesus paid a price he did not owe. He was never sinful and therefore could pay a debt we could not escape.

Jesus is the recipient of God's wrath for evil in the world. How, then, does God end the evil in us? Death stops the evil that has taken root in our world. The death of man will stop its spread. Men have known the truth but have not lived by it. As a result it must stop.

Jesus' life and death reveal, in a brand new way, the sinfulness of mankind. Paul says that men suppress the truth by their "wickedness." The word for wickedness (adikia) is injustice. It is humanity's injustice that suppresses the truth. Jesus reveals God's righteousness and human injustice through his perfect life and death. When people die, it is Jesus who judges.

I frequently find this principle at work among children. No matter what age a child is, you always have to filter what they say about their parents or teachers. I was a teacher for a year at a private Christian school in Dallas. When I first started, it was my impression that one teacher in particular was on some kind of power trip.

The reason I thought this wasn't because of any personal experience I had with the teacher. Instead, it was the vast number of students that came into my room and told me outlandish stories of the persecution in this classroom. My first thought was, *Well, if so many are saying this, it must have some merit to it.* However, I soon realized that mine was a faulty assumption.

As a young teacher, I often underestimated students' ability to place blame. I thought that the apparent inequity spread amongst so many people incriminated the teacher. What I realized later was that the uni-

ontml**32 | ANDREW B. HEARD**

formity of complaint didn't incriminate the teacher, instead it incriminated the students! It was the few students that did what they were asked to do and took full responsibility for their actions that helped me to see where the guilt laid. Jesus is like the good student who proves where the incrimination falls - not on God, but on the ones incriminated by their own charges.

It never fails that there are always those that see Jesus, yet still say it isn't their fault that they sin. Often people argue that they aren't guilty because they didn't know what was right. Paul knows this and hears the voices of opposition to his statement of judgment even before they are uttered. He knows that men try to pass the blame for their evil and therefore makes it clear that they can't. Paul tells the Romans that God is apparent in creation. Even those who are gentiles, and have lived without the Law, are guilty.

Paul is appealing here to what theologians call the natural law and logos spermatikos. Logos spermatikos says that in Christ are the building blocks of all creation. Since God created the world and did so through Christ, one can know something of God just by observing his creation.

According to Paul, God's divine nature is obvious to humanity. Here, Paul is explaining the moral Law. He wants the Romans to realize that they have always known right from wrong. They may have argued about the specifics, but everyone in the world has a concept of right and wrong in their society. By knowing that there is a right and wrong, they admit knowing of God's character.

People often disagree about what is right and wrong. In some societies suicide is a badge of honor, while in others it is a sin of damnation. How is it that these apparent contradictions help people to know God?

Paul isn't saying that everyone agrees on what is right and wrong. He is saying that everyone has a concept of them. Since we know there is right and wrong, we acknowledge that we know God. The universality of this shows us God is the root from which morality grows. The fact that we distort what right is doesn't mean that we don't know there is a right. Knowing that there is a right shows our guilt.

The Romans, just like many of us, know of God's character, but that knowledge cannot save them. They have no excuse for their sin because they know there is a correct conduct. They are without excuses. They are guilty and so are we.

I play basketball with our youth in the church league. I discovered something about myself recently that I find very upsetting. I can't jump. There was a time when I had a 37 inch vertical leap, but now it is more like 7 inches.

This decrease in athleticism is very upsetting. I have tried to blame everything for being out of shape. Often I'll say it's because I'm married or that I work too much. However, the more I go through the options, the more I realize there is no excuse.

There are simple laws at work in my inability to jump. If I work out and eat well, I will be in good shape. If I sit around and drink Dr. Pepper, I won't be in good shape. Who I am is about what I do. When I do the things that reap fat, I become fat. I can't jump because I choose to do the things (or to not do the things) that make me who I am.

Are you making excuses about who you are? Are you listing out the reasons why it's okay for you to commit your favorite sin? Humans have the ability to excuse anything. We tell ourselves that is it not our fault and then blame it on someone else.

There are all sorts of ways we place blame. Some of us blame our shortcomings on our parents. We say that if they only loved us more, or if they only spent more time with us, then we wouldn't act the way we do. The truth is the actions of our parents or anyone else matter little. We can't control the situations of our lives - we can only control the way we respond to the situations of our lives. Dr. Van K.Tharp, the professional trading coach and founder of the Van Tharp Institute, put it this way: "Most people would rather be in control, and be wrong, than feel the anxiety of having no control over the environment in which they must exist. The big step is in realizing that 'I have control over my actions.' And that is enough!"

Some of us don't place blame, we just deflect it. This is probably the most common response for teenagers. As teenagers, we find ourselves in an interesting position between childhood and adulthood. We want to do what we want and not take responsibility for our lives. We look at the people around us and judge how good or bad we are by their lives.

Walking into a high school and deciding how good or bad you are by the behavior of those around you is like having AIDS and deciding you are not really sick because the other people with AIDS look way worse than you do. You're not healthy just because you look better at the moment. AIDS and sin both kill you no matter how much better you think you look than someone else.

As humans we are sick. There is no excuse for our sin. We are sinful because we have chosen to be that way and, as a result, our sin deserves punishment. The punishment for your sin and my sin is the same. We deserve to die.

The reason we deserve death isn't an arbitrary decision by our creator. We don't deserve death because God is mad at us. Feeling that way about God and our punishment misses the point about the real travesty of our sin. Instead, how can we reject the giver of life and still expect to keep on living? Who has the power to sustain themselves? Who can give themselves breath or even a place to breathe? Without God we are without life and when we sin we are asking to be without God.

In Genesis, chapter three, Adam and Eve fall into sin by taking the forbidden fruit that they erroneously thought would give them wisdom. Instead of seeking wisdom by worshiping the creator, they looked to creation for their wisdom and in doing so dove into darkness. They looked at God, the creator of the world, and said, "I will do what I want in the world you created for me."

Because humans asked to live their lives without God, God let them. In Genesis 3:24, 26 and 28 the Bible says that God gave them over to their desires. In each circumstance, humans wanted to live apart from God and that apartness led them into destruction.

Sin destroyed them sexually, mentally, and emotionally. It destroyed them sexually by ripping away the very reasons for sex and the intimacy that should accompany it. Sin caused humanity to think incorrectly. People could not judge what was right. It destroyed them emotionally in that they couldn't love what they should. The human desire for independence resulted in people doing evil things.

Have humans realized they are the villains of their own story? If people are the villains, then they need a hero. Though we are guilty, God paved a way for us to be freed of our guilt.

While there is more complexity to this conversation, it is important to take a hard look at ourselves when looking to God. For the past eleven years I have dedicated my life to God. When I was young I struggled with pornography; I have preached sermons during a time when I didn't know if I believed; the other night I yelled at my wife while on Chemo because she said she didn't believe she was good enough to call herself a writer; I let Ellie (our eighteen-month-old) take a lollipop to the bathtub even though I knew she'd probably pee in the water and then dunk her lollipop before sucking on it again. Oh, and I love *Harry Potter*.

Like everyone, parts of me are good and white, parts are gray, and other parts smell bad and come out brown. Most humans are more like me than like Jesus. This is something to keep in mind as we struggle to understand our lives and our relationship with God.

CHAPTER 3

Doubting the Church

I recently watched an interview with a female pop star that I'll never forget. What became imprinted on my memory was the path the young lady took to stardom along with her thoughts on religion.

Katy Perry is one of the most successful singers to have emerged in the past few years. While singers come and go these days like facial hair on a youth minister, this young lady seems special. She is not only talented, she is also controversial.

One of Perry's more controversial songs is titled "I kissed a girl and I liked it." The song, which did quite well, has homosexual overtones in its lyrics which have caused a little bit of a stir. The fact that someone in the music industry wrote a song that was controversial is not surprising. It wasn't until I listened to Katy's television interview that I thought anything about her song.

In the interview, the reporter asked Katy about her life growing up. Katy grew up in a very conservative household. In fact, Katy's parents are very committed Christians. The fact that she grew up in the church and then fell away from her faith was somewhat of a shock to me.

Katy wasn't just someone that fell away from the faith. She actually started her career as a Christian artist and used her musical talent to serve God. However, now her music is far from God-glorifying. In the interview it sounded like just another story of someone losing faith in the church and moving out into the world.

What shocked me was what came next. Katy was showing the interviewer a tattoo of a Christian symbol when the reporter asked her what the symbol meant. I expected her to say something about how she just liked it, but that isn't close to what she said. Instead, Katy looked at the reported and said, "It reminds me that I can always go back, if I want to."

There is something about someone saying out loud what Katy Perry said. While she acknowledged going a different way, and understood that there was a way back, she was choosing not to go back to her faith. It hit me that this was a young lady that received love in the Christian community, yet turned her back on it. She obviously wasn't hostile toward the church even though it was no longer where she wanted to be.

Not everyone sees the church as a place that they can go back to. Many see the church as a place that would not allow them to return to after falling away. While most churches aren't hostile to people in a vocal manner, they can show people in nonverbal ways a judgment that is repelling. It is a bit hard to describe because using an extreme illustration wouldn't do justice to the problem. Judgment by the church happens in such extreme measures that it often causes people to be jaded toward organized religion for the rest of their lives.

Judgment in the American church happens in an "American Idol" sort of way. We choose who is worthy of our attention, laugh at some, and never let others make the show. I remember what happened to a young man I grew up with. I'll call him Victor.

Victor was a young African American who played sports with me. We did a lot of things together from the time we were little. He was a person with a genuinely sweet spirit. As I think back, I wish we had been even better friends.

I invited Victor to join a few sports leagues with me, which he did. However, I never asked him to come to church with me. Part of this was due to my lack of spiritual depth at the time. Growing up, I didn't see either my faith or myself very clearly. I'm still not sure that I see myself that well, though I do have a better understanding of Christianity. At the time, I wasn't very mature and didn't know how to invite people of different races to church.

I did not grow up in a racist hick town, and my church wasn't full of racist hicks. There were many loving people in the church and race was never spoken of in a derogatory manner. While no overt attempt was made to keep certain people away, few people of other races attended.

After having served in different sized churches in other places, I realize what happened at my home church is what happens most everywhere. As has been said many times, Sunday morning is the most segregated time in America. Churches tend to be places where you go to be around others who look like us, be they white, black or Asian. Though there are exceptions here and there, in general, this is our reality.

What is often heard about segregated churches is that people group together because that is where they feel most comfortable. I hear this kind of talk when I am around church leaders and see its validity. The point is that we tend to reach the people we are most suited to reach. While I understand this train of thought, and don't feel it is necessarily evil, I often ask myself why certain people don't feel comfortable in our churches.

Our judgment does not come down in overt measures employed by organizations like the Ku Klux Klan. Instead, our judgment is through association with people who seem worthy while ostracizing those we judge not to be deserving of our attention. This is hardest for me because it is true in my life. Where or whom to spend my time with is the greatest struggle of my day. As we get older there are more conflicts that steal my time. We only have so many hours in a day and where we spend them is very important.

Jesus spent much of his time tearing down the walls of judgment. The Gospels are littered with examples of Jesus healing the sick. Have you ever wondered why healing was so important to Jesus? Taken at face value, it doesn't make much sense. Why does Jesus heal the physical bodies when he was more concerned with their soul? Why does he bother to heal so many people? What lesson is he teaching? Many times Jesus heals people and then tells them not to tell anyone. If he isn't concerned with making himself known and isn't leading them out to be baptized after their healing, why is it so important to him that the sick are healed? If it's not about eternity, why does it matter?

We don't think of the sick as people to stay away from. If someone has a contagious disease, we might ask them not to come to work for a while. However, we still talk to them on the phone and when they are better they can come to church or hang out with us whenever they want. In ancient society, sickness was thought of very differently. There was no science or medicine to cure disease the way we do now. Instead, people saw sickness as judgment and uncleanness. In Jesus' day those with chronic disease were excluded from society and public events like worship. Sick people were judged as unclean and kept at arm's length. They were not stoned, instead they were just left outside the city where no one paid attention to them. But they weren't just left outside the city, they were also left outside the Temple. They were left outside the place they could encounter God - God's presence was not open to them.

We should not run from people because they struggle with sin. Everyone struggles with sin. If we can't admit that, then we are liars and the truth is not in us. The distinction between people is one of the heart. Does the person struggling desire to be different? Are they trying, even in the smallest extent, but unable to overcome? These are the people God calls us to share our burden with. We are to walk hand in hand with them, lift them up and even carry them when they can't walk.

There are people who are in willful sin and have no desire to repent. These are people Paul calls us to no longer associate with in the hope they will be brought to repentance. This is something that is hardly ever done in the church. When it is, it is not usually done in a godly manner. I think it is because we are so touched by our own sin that we can't fathom punishing someone else. If we are ever going to carry out God's command without judgment, we have to raise our own standards in our walk with God.

Holding a standard, but not sinking into condemning judgment, is tied to the principle of loving others. If we fully love others, we won't ostracize them. Nor will we ignore the sin that destroys the redeemed soul. Here is the key: "Have an honest conversation." Rather than judging someone and not talking to them, take them out for a drink. Confront them with honesty by saying: "Hey man, what's the deal about you cheating on your wife?" Or maybe you invite your business partner out for lunch and ask him why he is drinking so much. The problem is that most of us don't care enough about others to have an earnest and loving conversation. We don't need to kick people out of our company to achieve what Paul was wanting. If we have the conversation, people will either get ticked off and remove themselves from our company or they will ask for help.

The Bible says we should approach the conversation with unbelievers differently. This is something so many in the church need to grasp. We have problems in our hearts that need to be healed. My mother-in-law puts it very well when she says, "Don't judge people's outsides by your insides." She is telling us not to think that others are so different from us based on what we see on the outside. We all have a way of masking who we really are by the way we act on the outside. Neither can we perceive who people really are by what we see at a distance. We can't feel better or worse by comparing ourselves to others. The judgment about who we are comes from God and no one else.

The conservative evangelical church which I consider myself part of has poured judgment out on the world far too often. Rather than protecting the innocent, it has revealed its own piety.

Have you seen the political messages against those who are gay in the past ten years? They are often movements led by Christians who say we must protect the moral fiber of our country because we are a Christian nation. They say homosexuals can't be married because marriage is meant for a man and a woman. As a result, they have rallied the Christian body to vote against gays and to tell them what they can and cannot have based on a Christian world view.

Have we forgotten Paul's words saying those who don't know Christ aren't held to the same standards that Christians are? We are not to pour judgment out on sinners. If we do, it shows that we don't understand our own salvation. Do we believe that we saved ourselves? Do we think we could be different without the help of Christ? Those who think those things would benefit from reading the book of Romans. The idea that we can be right without God's help was called heresy in the early church. If you think you become more like God on your own, then Plagius, the ancient heretic, is alive and well within you.

Inappropriate judgment is found when we ask others to hold onto a standard without love. There is no love in abusing the unredeemed for being who they are. The gay community doesn't need our judgment. They have plenty of that themselves. Instead, the gay community needs God's love in the same way that we do. They will not feel loved it if we keep them at arm's length by mandating their actions through political power.

The church does not extend its influence through the voting booth. Nor is the church stronger because the president is a Christian. Caesar is not lord, Christ is Lord. When we decide to change the world through political power, we give up our rights to the power of the Gospel. The Gospel calls us to change people by serving them, not by telling them what to do. Jesus didn't change the lives of sinners by enacting laws to stop them from sinning. That is what the Pharisees did. They are the ones that said people should worship God on the Sabbath and then put laws into effect that punished those who wouldn't obey them.

Think about the sins you struggled with before you became a Christian. Perhaps you have been a Christian so long that you can't remember them. If so, think about the sins you have struggled with since becoming a Christian. What if I, as a pastor, had laws passed that said you couldn't be with your family anymore if you struggled with sin? Would you come to me wanting to know Jesus because you were kept from doing what you were involved in? Maybe if you knew Jesus, you would. However, if it was before you knew Jesus, you would probably resent me.

What if you didn't know Jesus and were living in deep sin with your life in shambles? What if I were there for you when things were bad? What if I were to wash your feet and heal your wounds? Maybe then, maybe if I loved you and served you, you would open your heart to the love of a God who wants to walk with you.

The church often tells gays that they aren't loved and that it wants to control their actions without loving them enough to be their friend. The actions of the church are pushing the unbeliever away while holding close to those who know Jesus, yet despise his calling. We are doing exactly what Christ told us not to do.

If you are a homosexual reading this book, I want you to know that I hurt for you in your struggle. I am sorry that the world has put you in a situation where you are being hurt. I can see that it affects your ability to have a family and causes you to struggle with your identity. While I may not understand your struggle, I want you to know that I love you and that Christ loves you. This book wasn't written specifically to help you with your situation. It was written to help those who should love you the most to stop acting in ways that they shouldn't.

There are some of you that are angry with me for not acknowledging the detriment to society presented by same-sex marriages. The biggest detriment to society is when we stoop loving others. Do you have a gay neighbor you are worried about? Why not become their best friend? Then you can talk to them about what you think! But until then, keep your mouth shut and love someone to Jesus.

America, which is a Christian nation, does not depend on the government for teaching morality. This has traditionally been the job of the church. But Jesus is not just about morality. If you want to simply follow a moral code to redemption, pick another religion. Jesus came to help the sick, not the healthy. We are a Christian nation because the church teaches its people to follow our Lord. This, however, doesn't happen by simply pushing people around within its voting block.

Is the government creating an atmosphere in which the church is free to do her job? Is it protecting life, liberty, and property? Is it a nation where people are free? Are its people free to accept Christ or to turn from him? America has an obligation to ensure the freedom of its people. Does that mean that the people have the right to take certain freedoms away because an activity is distasteful?

Do you want your child to grow up in a world where homosexual activity is flaunted? If you don't, then go find your gay neighbor and love them. I admit this is something I've not done as well as I should. Personally I don't know many homosexual people. Perhaps I need to be more intentional. Those I have met, I don't understand very well and often feel awkward around. But Jesus didn't call us to something easy, he called us to the cross.

The good news is that we don't have to do it alone or with judgment. The idea of judgment is something that can get a little gray. How do we hold people to a standard and not judge them? I can't provide an exact path, but I can tell you that it involves doing things in love. Will you join me in loving a world that suffers from judgment?

I have some real doubts about whether the American church can make this transition. Many churches are oriented toward judgment. It is something that makes me want to vomit. As a minister I have felt that judgment. It is important we get to the root of this issue. Why can't the church go out and love the world without causing the judgment that is so rampant?

CHAPTER 4

Doubting Who Goes to Heaven

Prior to finding out that I had stage four lung cancer, I realized that I was depressed. I was so depressed that I decided to quit the ministry. On most Saturdays I would have panic attacks in anticipation of Sunday morning.

I told my executive pastor about my struggle. He not only was encouraging, he also helped me find a therapist. Many Christians avoid therapy because they feel like being depressed means they aren't true to their faith. This is wrong minded. If you are depressed, get help for your illness because that is what it is. You aren't a bad believer because you are depressed; you just have a chemical problem and need help.

I sucked up my pride and went to get help. The therapist, who had degrees from well-known schools and was well thought of in Dallas, seemed to be very good. We met for about five weeks and things seemed to be going really well. I would enter his office, sit on his nice leather couch, and then watch as he would take my blood pressure prior to starting our session. He had a great therapist beard (very Freudian-esk) which I thought was interesting. Before starting, I would always stare at his book collection. It is interesting what you learn by the books someone reads.   Much of our session time focused on my theological problems and feelings about God. The therapist asked good questions. One week in particular was interesting. He asked me to think about all my questions and what would happen if my questions turned out to have bad answers. Then to accept those bad answers.

I went home and thought through my questions. What if my answers were bad? Would I go to hell as a result? Or, perhaps, maybe a lot of people I love might go to hell. I followed the therapist's orders and meditated on them for a week. As a result, it was one crappy week. The next week, he asked what I decided. I told him and we both decided that it was pretty bad. Then he stared at me. I assumed that he was using some kind of therapist voodoo on me.

It was the next visit that really set me off. I was discussing a service I had led at church involving an interactive sermon with my students that upset me. At one point, I'd asked them what happened to Gandhi after he died. It got pretty heated and some of the adults in the room became upset with me because I hadn't given the kids any resolution to the question. That was done on purpose, since I thought it was a question that needed to be thoughtfully considered. Though Gandhi wasn't a professing Christian, it couldn't be denied that he did works for humankind. As Christians, how do we deal with that? Gandhi lived a lot like I believe Jesus would have wanted him to, but he didn't have a public profession of faith… So, what happens to him? I said that while I didn't know, I hoped for something good.

My therapist seemed irritated with me. Pushing me further, I stood my ground about Gandhi. He asked me to clarify my own beliefs. I stated that Jesus brought salvation, but wasn't sure how it worked or exactly who he was. Then my therapist said the words that caused me to leave his practice. "Maybe *you* are going to hell." Laughing, I thought he was joking. Instead, he stared weirdly at me. I said, "I don't think I'm going to hell." He replied, "you might go to hell!"

This story is a perfect example of what we have made of religion. This man had less theological training than me. He clearly didn't have any understanding of the issues, yet he was sure he could judge me. I am amazed at what many people believe about religion. Having served at three large churches in the Dallas area, I think many feel we are the "have it your way generation." There is a spoof on the Burger King ad campaign that illustrates this perfectly.

The clip features a comedian by the name of BonQuiQui who plays a cashier at Burger King based on their ad campaign. Burger King is thought to be the place where you can have it your way, however, Bon-QuiQui hasn't completely bought into it. She sees customer after customer and dismisses many of them because their orders are too complicated. BonQuiQui changes the line from "have it your way" to "welcome to Burger King where you can have it your way, but don't get crazy."

Have it your way, but don't get crazy, is exactly how we tend to look at God. I watch as students and parents go from church to church looking for something that is made their way. If they don't like something at one church, they try another. If they are confronted with their sin by one group, they march on to the next group of people. They might be looking for the next youth event or a great speaker without thinking twice about whether or not this is what God intended. In doing so, we risk changing the core message about what church was intended to be. We want it our way, but we don't want to live crazily for the needs of others. Instead, we try to make our God exactly like we want him. We don't want him to be too big or ask very much of us. Rather, we just want him to help us feel better and let us do what we want. The reason I know about this is because I see it every day and I have done it myself.

Voltaire was an ancient French philosopher who put it perfectly when he said, "If God has made us in his image, we have returned him the favor".[1] If you need a modern version of Voltaire, look no further than the great work of the philosopher Will Ferrell in the movie *Talladega Nights: The Ballad of Ricky Bobby*. There is a very funny scene in the movie where Ricky Bobby's family is sitting down to a delicious fast-food dinner. In the scene, Bobby's wife, Carley Bobby, asks him to say grace.

The prayer he gives is downright hysterical. Although many people took offense to the movie when it first came out, Ricky Bobby gives a pretty accurate depiction of the way many Christians think about Christ. Here is what takes place as Ricky Bobby recites the family prayer:

"Dear Lord Baby Jesus, or as our brothers in the south call you, 'hesus.' We thank you so much for this bountiful harvest of Domino's, KFC and the always delicious Taco Bell."

After giving thanks for his family and asking the Lord to heal his dog's leg, Ricky Bobby ends the prayer with a mention of his sponsor, Powerade, saying that it is in his contract to make mention of them while praying. In his prayer he refers to Jesus as "Eight pound, six ounce, newborn baby Jesus."

We aren't the only ones who have ever struggled with wanting to make Jesus only 6 pounds 8 ounces.

Are there people in your world so self-consumed that they believe the world is created around their lives or that God is just a little better than them? Some people can act like idiots. The story of this world is so much bigger than just one church's statement of belief. The story of this world is about the glory and faithfulness of an almighty God who enters the world of the fallen to save the hopeless.

Are you one of those who think that we save yourselves? If so, I am happy to say you are wrong. There is nothing you can do to make yourself right with God. Salvation has nothing to do with you and everything to do with Jesus. He is not asking you to be a little better nor to

---

[1] Wikipedia 'Voltaire' Notebooks (c.1735-c.1750)

control yourself more. He is asking you to give up control.

God knows that you are incapable of controlling yourself. Many pray the same prayer about avoiding cursing or gossiping. If you are, you are missing the heart of the Gospel. God doesn't want you to clean yourself up so he can love you. Instead, he dirtied himself so that you can love him. It's when we fall in love with our savior and pull close to him that he removes the sin in our life. When struggling with sin we have to pray that the illusions of this world fade as God causes us to fall more and more in love with him.

I have had some conversations lately that really make me think about my western, individualist mindset. There is a question that many Americans ask that people in eastern cultures would never ask. Western children often ask themselves, why did God allow me to be born into this family? You may be wondering why I think it is a strange question. I think it's strange because the more appropriate question is not asked. Shouldn't the child instead ask, "Why has my family chosen this path?" "Why has my family chosen to be Muslim or Christian?" When we ask why God has placed us in the family we live in, we create a disconnect between ourselves and the family we belong to. We also make ourselves the victim of God's arbitrary decision making. Western children see themselves as individuals and autonomous from their families.

We think we were some preexistent being that God took from the heavens and placed in our family. The truth is, our identity is due to our family. My disposition, my hair color, my walk, even my teeth are the way they are because I am the son of my mother and father. My existence can't be separated from their lives. We in the western world are quick to forget this.

We are a part of a family that differs from our biological parents. In Romans, Paul points out the faithfulness of Jesus to the covenant and his faith to trust God with his death on the cross eliminated the alienation of gentiles. Jews, for so long, thought that God only brought truth and hope to them because they were the chosen people. They thought they were his only people. In Romans Paul tells them that God is also the God of the gentiles. God, through the sacrifice of his son, has revealed his faithfulness to the people of the whole world. Paul needed the Romans to see that God was not just in it for a certain group of people, but for all people. The Jews thought that the Law put religion in their control. However, as much as religion tries to control God, it never can. Paul wants the Romans to know that through Jesus' death and resurrection that his power has been released in order to bring about a new family. A faith that can't be controlled. A family that, through the Spirit of God, forcefully entered our world.

Are you struggling to control who can be part of God's family? Perhaps you are thinking, *I would never say that someone couldn't be a part of the church.* Though we may say that, why do we only share Jesus with a certain group of people? Do we only extend invitations to those who follow the rules or follow the law?

When was the last time you reached out to someone who was unchurched? Someone who made you feel uncomfortable? It is very hard for me as well. It is for a number of reasons. It is hard because people who don't follow "our" rules aren't comfortable to talk with. We don't understand each other. Some of us have been in the church for so long that we no longer know how to talk to the unchurched.

The other reason why it is so hard to reach out to the unchurched is simple. We don't care if they meet Jesus. While we may say that we care while in Sunday school or cry when someone walks into our church and gives their life to Jesus, we don't care enough to purposefully live our lives so that people who don't know the love of God… Let's face it, getting involved in people's lives can be messy and sometimes involves emotional garbage. Reaching out interrupts our schedule and can tarnish our reputations.

I know this is all true because I feel it in my own life. But when I ask myself what Jesus died for, it becomes easier. The apostle Paul says that Jesus died so that there would be a worldwide family of faith and that there would be no difference between the Jews and Gentiles. He died so that the people who didn't know the rules would have a chance to be with God. Jesus died in order for people who couldn't follow the rules could have eternal life. He wanted everyone to have the chance at life, even those who don't look like us. If Jesus died for the world to be a family of faith, why can't we reach out to our brothers and sisters?

Reaching out to others isn't easy. You must first let go of control, which isn't easy. It requires us to have help from God and the support of a family of faith.

The church was created to be your family of faith. A family that is more like you than any earthly family could ever be. You are bonded with the Spirit of God when you are a part of a church. Churches aren't perfect. While churches aren't perfect, they are a place where people are committed to try to let go of control. Having someone to walk beside you in the process of reaching out to the world is essential. It is there to protect you.

Are you struggling to make God what you want him to be? Why do you have to have him your way? It is not about you! To live the life God has purchased for us, we have to realize that it's not about us.

Instead, it needs to be about someone else. We discussed reaching out to the "unchurched" in the world. This can involve making friends with people who believe differently than we do. It doesn't mean forcing them to believe what we believe. While the Old Testament told of forcing the Kingdom of God into existence through violence, the New Testament is different.

Relax. Jesus saved the world so you don't have to. You just need to love those you encounter in the world. Sometimes we can get so busy saving the world that we forget to love those in it.

When you stop loving the world and start forcing the world to believe what you do, it makes one want to say what I wanted to say to that therapist: "Screw you. Maybe *you're* going to hell." But those aren't the words of a Christ follower. If someone is having a crisis of faith, we need to love them and remind them that Christ came into the world so that they could have that crisis. If others don't share our faith, we love them because Christ had faith.

As one who is dying, I am encountering God in amazing ways every day. Even so, I am so confused theologically that I can barely see straight, and yet God still makes his face known to me. If God is doing that for me, then he will be there for all all who are hurting and confused. I don't know if it will be in this life or the next, but he will be there for them.

If you think you have all the answers and can stand on knowledge before love, then I hope you enjoy the role of High Priest and wish you the best with slaughtering cattle. If this is for you, then be careful not to be closer to BonQuiQui than to that of a leader of God's people.

CHAPTER 5

Depression and Hope

There are some who feel a Christian cannot be depressed. Others think it is a spiritual deficiency. I say those people are misinformed. The fact is, life is hard. I have felt pretty depressed the last few days in spite of being on antidepressant medications the past two years. It took a year and a half to find a medication that helped me. Taking that medicine has made my life so much better.

There was a time when going to church depressed me so much that I would have anxiety attacks. Nothing was particularly wrong at work or in other areas of my life. Though I had some theological struggles and coworker issues, there was nothing so bad that it should have caused anxiety attacks.

There is a history of depression in my family that also affected me.

I went to the therapist and tried different solutions but nothing really helped. It took a major life change and new medicine for me to begin the recovery process.

Did my bout with depression make me a bad Christian? During that time I also questioned God. Does that mean I was straying from God's path? When we ask these questions, there are some important things to consider. Humans are comprised of more than just spirit and soul. We are body, spirit, and soul. Those elements combine in a way that we don't fully understand. When someone has a mental breakdown we don't consider them sinful, even if they become a different person and run through the halls of a hospital naked. Instead we understand that something has happened in their body that has altered their ability to control how they relate to the world.

I believe depression can be seen in much the same light. When I am down emotionally, it affects my body. My spirit and soul remain the same. Recently I was denied treatment using a new trial drug for lung cancer. The news made me feel depressed. Did I sin by becoming sad and depressed? Does it show my lack of faith? Absolutely not.

Jesus cried out to God in the garden before his crucifixion and sweated blood because of anxiety. He didn't sin due to having anxiety. However, he clearly felt stress and was physically affected to the point that the capillaries in his sweat glands burst.

Maybe you don't sweat blood, but perhaps you can't sleep or have depression that you can't seem to beat. Having depression doesn't make you a bad Christian. It's okay to ask for help. As humans, it is okay to take medicine and talk to a therapist.

I have cancer, and sometimes I am mad about it. Other times I am sad and have to cry. The other night my wife rubbed my back as I cried. My chances of surviving the cancer I have is only four percent. I think about my beautiful daughter and wife and lose it because I don't want to miss out on their lives. My daughter Ellie may never know me.

If I cry because my chances of living to see her grow up are so low, it doesn't mean I don't have faith. My faith helps me to believe that I will see my daughter again one day. I have faith that my life doesn't end if I die this year. I believe God will forgive me of my sins because of my faith in Jesus.

My faith in God is deep, even though sometimes I get sad and struggle with depression. There will be a day when I don't sin anymore or struggle with depression. Jesus loves me in the midst of my struggles. We live in a world where it is hard to see the love of Christ through all the tragedy and hardship.

Thoughtful Christians know that people need hope to survive. This is true for Christians and non-Christians. Our world doesn't turn without hope.

The world suffers from depression. We have seen how far humanity can fall. The evil of Auschwitz, bigotry in Africa, the face of selfishness in abortion, etc. We see the hurt of humanity all around us.

I recently read a story online that put my stomach in knots. *Daily News* reporter Dana Bartholomew reported on a story of a young girl in Indonesia named Yulce who grew up with her family in a bamboo hut on a remote island. As a Christian living in a Muslim community, she was already somewhat of an outcast. What happened to her one day changed her world forever.

Yulce was sitting in her hut when the kerosene lamp used to light the room started to run low, so she got up to refill it. Suddenly the lamp exploded, covering Yulce with kerosene.

Yulce received third degree burns on her face, neck, chest, and upper arms. Without medical care she suffered with horrible pain for six months. As she finally started to heal, the scars melted her face into her chest, her lower lip vanished, her ears disappeared, and her arms were fused to her side.

When people in her village saw Yulce, they told her mother, "Your daughter is dead, put her outside." Friends who once played with Yulce now teased her. As a result, Yulce refused to leave her hut and felt despair.[2]

How can someone like Yulce have hope? At such a young age, so much was taken from this little girl and she suffered miserably. How can Christians tell her that she should have hope? Most of us don't have scars like Yulce, but that doesn't mean we don't carry other kind of scars. One of the most common scars I see people carrying comes from their families.

Many children suffer from despair because of the actions of their parents. How do we tell children to have hope when they have watched their parents rip each other apart either verbally or physically? Telling them to rejoice when they are tossed back and forth between parents having to go from one house to another each weekend is discouraging.

Have you ever notice how churches have different styles of worship? Often they vary wildly from church to church. One church, where people are set free and rejoicing flows from their souls, will see dancing and crying during the same song. Some worship services allow us to actually feel the presence of the Holy Spirit.

Then there are other churches where many feel awkward. You hear the minister announce a song of worship but, looking around, not everyone is participating. It is important to understand that it isn't the style of worship that guides the experience of hope during worship. I have preached in nursing homes where we didn't even have a piano, yet the worship was deep because we sang the hymns that people could remember.

I have also been in worship services that were filled with strobe lights and the newest, hippest worship songs, yet the worship wasn't rejoicing. You can feel when a congregation is singing about God's activity among them. If you have been in the room of authentic worship that rejoices at the activity of God among the people, you probably have left saying how wonderful it was.

I am not speaking of emotional worship, even though emotion is important. Rather, I am talking about rejoicing at God's redemptive work

[2] http://www.thefreelibrary.com/ONE+GIRL'S+THANKSGIVING+STORY+FROM+DESPAIR+TO+HOPE-a0125360135

among his people. Worship through song is a product of life when it has been touched by God. We don't sing because we have to, we sing because we can't help it.

Most of us think of the glory of God and picture Jesus with long, flowing hair just washed with Herbal Essence appearing in the sky with some gold, designer bathrobe. For others of us, GQ Jesus isn't where we see God's glory. Instead, we see it through those we've encountered. It might be the coach who used the paddle as a means of authority. When we think about God displaying his glory, we think God has his heavenly paddle ready to come down and spank all the bad kids who don't honor him the way they should.

When I was in student ministry, intimidation was the paddle most often used as the instrument of God's glory. Students asked how much they could do before God got mad. This question is one of the saddest questions in ministry. It is especially sad to me because I remember asking it.

When students ask this question, there is no hope in their heart. They aren't thinking of what God might help them to become - they are thinking about what they can do to hide who they are. This is a hopeless idea because we cannot hide who we are from God. It is discouraging to find that our religion is disguising what fills our heart. It is something that we must repent of because it is not the message of hope we have in Jesus.

The world doesn't need another religion that asks people to cover up who they are. That kind of hypocrisy makes others want to pity or condemn the Christian. There is no hope or power in diluted people who are acting as if they have been changed.

If you are not walking with Jesus, I want you to know that hypocrisy is not what our savior intended. He wanted us to have hope. Hope is something that helps us to believe what we will have one day. Christianity doesn't set you free from mistakes. Instead, it makes you realize that, with God's help, you can overcome and grow past the wrongs you have committed. It can take time, and it is not an easy fix, but we don't have to fear our mistakes because Christ will help us overcome them.

The Bible tells us to rejoice in our suffering. There are many Christians that do ridiculous things. You know who I am talking about. They are the ones that lost their job and were bitten by a dog the same week but can't stop smiling. You look at this poor guy and say, "I am so sorry. That must have been really hard on you." Immediately you get a cheesy smile follwed by, "God has blessed me by being attacked by a dog and losing my job. I can't tell you how happy I am."

In the words of my wife's favorite tween star, "Crazy church boy say what?" I think the apostle Paul would agree with me when I say to lay off this kind of thinking. We don't rejoice that we suffer, we rejoice that suffering produces something more in us. Paul says that suffering produces endurance and endurance produces character.

God is changing us. Our suffering is a tool that he can use. He wants us to endure the trials of this life because as we do, we have a chance to grow. Endurance is something that helps us to prove that we trust God. Saying we trust without being tested doesn't require much trust.

A person who has been tested tends to have character. When we stand firm in our beliefs we show character. It allows us to see God at work in our day-to-day life.

I read a story this week about a guy named Todd Carmichael. Todd is a native of Philadelphia, but his story starts about as far away from Philly as possible. He is an adventurer and his lust for adventure took him to one of the coldest places on earth.

Todd became obsessed with breaking the world record for the fastest land crossing of Antarctica. Even after reading the article, I am still not sure why this particular record appealed to Todd so much, but it did.

The first time Todd set out to break the record, he ended up having to be picked up by a helicopter and flown home. The harsh elements of the South Pole had become too much for him. Failure has a weird way of either pushing us forward to great successes our destroying us.

Todd was sucked into destruction for a time after his failure in Antarctica. He describes how he was gripped by depression because of the loss of his dream. What is amazing is that Todd didn't stop and didn't stay in his depression. Instead, he picked himself up and went right back to Antarctica.

When Todd started his second journey across Antarctica, it didn't begin well. Soon he was over twenty hours behind the world record pace. He spent all day walking, only stopping to eat and sleep. Even eating 8,000 calories a day, Todd still lost over forty pounds on his journey.

Toward the end of the trek, Todd was still behind the pace, yet he wasn't concerned with the record any longer. His stove broke and he wasn't able to melt snow for hydration. To make matters worse, his satellite phone broke so he couldn't call for help. Even his GPS stopped working.

Todd was just a few miles from the base he was hiking to at the South Pole, but without his GPS he wasn't sure he would be able to find it. The day was unusually clear and Todd thought he could see the base in the distance.

He began to see hallucinations because of his lack of food and water. Not sure that he was really seeing what he hoped he was seeing, Todd left all his supplies behind and began to walk to the camp in the distance. He walked for two days straight to reach the base.

As Todd reached the airstrip at the base, he looked at his watch to see how far he was from the world record. In his delirium, Todd realized that he was just 2 hours ahead of the world record.

The trials and anxiety of his trip had pushed him farther than he could have ever predicted and helped him to achieve something that he never thought he would at the beginning of his trip. The doctors that attended to Todd at the camp said that he had about one more day before his lungs would shut down from frost-bite and he would have died. A few hours later, the area was covered in a snow-storm that cut visibility down to a quarter mile. A few hours later and Todd would have been dead.

I don't know if Todd is a believer or if he sees supernatural intervention in his story, but I am sure that he sees his trip as producing character in his life. I would guess that Todd never enjoyed those character-testing setbacks on his trip, but he has to look back now and see that they did show him much about character and perseverance. For those of us who know God, it is very easy to see God in Todd's story.

In the moments that test our character, God reveals himself. It is time-tested character that produces hope. When we have seen God at work in our lives, we can fully trust that he will finish the work he has started so that we will one day be all that we always should have been. It is overcoming obstacles in our lives that show us God's redemptive work.

Do you have hope? It can be so hard to have hope in this world. We are surrounded by so much hardship and we know that more suffering is to come. Yulce's mom knew that their suffering wasn't over. She knew that her daughter would suffer every day, and yet she told a reporter, "I kept praying and praying. I still picture my daughter the way she was before the fire."

Yulce's mom was willing to endure for her daughter and let her character be tested. In the midst of it, she rejoiced and cried out to God. Yulce's mother's cry didn't go unheard.

An Australian missionary working in Indonesia saw Yulce and her mother's situation and was moved to action. With the help of twelve doctors and a large grant, Yulce was brought to the world's best burn hospital. After numerous surgeries, Yulce is going to school and is happy. She joked with her mother, "I like school and it's not too hard. You can go home and I'll stay here." Yulce's mother told reporters, "This, to me, is a miracle. I looked at her picture before the surgery and it made me cry. Right now I look at her and she's got her arms, her lips, and her cheeks, I give thanks to God."

Yulce and her mother aren't through with their suffering. Yulce is not perfect, but she has hope. She has hope because she endured her sufferings, which brought her character. This character lets her know that God is at work in her life and he won't stop working until he has made her perfect.

How do we tell people to rejoice in their suffering? We tell them to let God work a little Yulce in them. We don't all get completely healed in this life, but it is the healing work of our Lord through all the small victories in our life that lets us hope. It is God's gift of the Holy Spirit never leaving us in the midst of our suffering that allows us to hope.

Let the Holy Spirit comfort you in the midst of your suffering. We all suffer. Some suffer to different degrees and in different ways, but we all encounter suffering and will continue to do so all our lives. Suffering bonds us. It is a common element to all humanity and in that commonality we have a bond of the soul.

You don't suffer alone. There are millions of people around the world who are suffering with you and a God that walks through that suffering with each one of us. Who is this God who suffers with us? He is our healer. By his suffering we have been healed. He who understands every pain does not see us without compassion.

Some lack hope because God has not been let in to treat the wounds. It is time to give up despair and let God's hope grip you. He will never leave you nor forsake you. He won't mock you and will always love you. That is the hope we have.

CHAPTER 6

The Death of Dreams

Recently the story of the abduction and release of Jaycee Lee Dugard has been in the news. Taken off the street at age eleven, this little girl was victimized for eighteen years before being rescued by authorities in the summer of 2009. Then twenty-nine with two daughters, who were allegedly fathered by her captor, Jaycee was finally reunited with her family. Miracles do indeed happen.

As we learned more about the things that happened during her long ordeal, we understand more about the incredible courage and determination of Jaycee. Just as with Shawn Hornbeck, who was held for four years before being rescued, Jaycee experienced a horror that few have endured.

After her rescue some people asked why she didn't escape when she had the chance. However, to answer the question requires an understanding about the power such a predator has over their victims. Imagine being controlled by a monster while being sexually assaulted and repeatedly brutalized. In many cases the captive is threatened with violent retaliation for any attempts to get away, including death or the death of loved ones. In many longer term cases, the abductees begin to relate to the abductor as the mind games and brainwashing influence the captive, not to mention the pure survival mode of finding ways to curry favor with the abductor to prevent future torture.[3]

Jaycee's story is horrible and most of us will never be able to relate to what she went through. However, there is one level in which we all relate to the captivity of Jaycee.

Captivity comes in many forms. The apostle Paul said, "The things I want to do, I don't do and the things I do are the very things I don't want to do." There are captives who are trapped in addiction, lost in lust, and shackled by heart break. Looking at our world and at my own life, I realize there were important questions I had to ask. Why am I this way? Why do I betray myself? Why am I not what I wanted to be?

Durring my third year of seminary, I was on the Baylor football team. On opening day we played TCU. It was everything a great college football day should be. The tailgaters were out and there was the smell of barbecue in the air. Banners were all flying from the stadium roof and music was thumping from the field.

I loved college football, but that day all I could do was cry. As we pulled up to the stadium in my parent's car I knew I belonged in the locker room with the rest of the team. The shame and disappointment overwhelmed me.

There had been a point in the spring when it looked like I would start at slot receiver. But then my groin gave way and everything changed.

[3] Child Rescue Network, "Jaycee Dugard Rescued"; available from http://www.childrescuenetwork. org/index.php?option=com_content&view=article&id=74:jaycee-dugard&catid=1:latest-news; Internet; accessed December 13, 2009.

Even though I tried all summer to rehab my sports hernia, when the season came I couldn't run. When a player is injured many times, you don't suit up. Instead, they watch the game from the players' section of the stands.

Sitting in my parent's car that day I knew I would never play college football. I was right. In my career, I played a total of six plays. I even took shots in my groin in order to try to play. However, my injury prevented me from running. It may sound silly getting so upset about football, but for me it was the loss of a dream. My entire life I dreamed of playing college football, but that day, sitting in my parent's car, my dream died.

I blamed God for the death of my dream, even though I'd been offered a medical redshirt which would have allowed me to play more years. However, I decided to turn it down because I believed God didn't want me to be successful playing football. Things had gone so well at first that I was sure God was with me. There were magazine and newspaper articles about me and I was preforming so well at practice and then it all fell apart. It felt so much like my senior year of high school when I broke my leg and got cancer. I assumed God was killing my dream and that I needed to accept it and move on.

The problem was, accepting it and moving on wasn't easy. How do you kill a childhood dream especially when it feels like it was God who killed it? I think a lot of people struggle with this question. Middle age men look back at their lives and have a crisis because they aren't where they thought they would be. Moms realize that their child has taken a terrible path in life after they did everything they could to love and nurture their child.

When a dream dies we can be taken captive by blame and hurt which can pull us in without seeing out. It's as if God lined the world up against us and it is too late to do anything about it. I grieved the loss of football for nearly five years after I graduated.

In our culture we don't like things that take time. Instead, we judge things by how quickly they can be delivered to us. The Internet, television, and fast food are all examples of things we judge by speed. If our Internet service isn't fast enough, we switch providers. If our food doesn't get to us fast enough, we find a different restaurant.

Recently AT&T came out with a new package called U-verse. The reason this package is so appealing is that you can record four television shows at one time on the same television set. This package is appealing to me for multiple reasons, but mostly due to speed. When Tevo first came out, I never understood the appeal. I even told our installation specialist that it was not a big deal if we didn't have a digital recorder. I can tell you now that I can't imagine not having digital recording capabilities.

The reason I love Tevo so much is that I can fly through all the commercials and watch only the things I like.

I have come to realize that many of us want a fast forward button on our life. We think that because we can skip all the parts of television, we wish that we can do it similarly with our spiritual lives. Here's a newsflash: "You can't Tevo God!"

Our generation has lost our appreciation for the process of character development. We don't know about the virtue of patience. Instead, we have decided to lift up progress as production and failed to realize that there may be great progress in struggling.

Athletes know that there is progress in the struggle. When an athlete trains for a sport, there are no shortcuts. You can't think your way to being faster. Developing strength takes time and requires struggling against so much weight that it threatens to crush you. Good athletes don't run away from that crushing weight or blame their coach for placing them under it. Instead, they embrace the process of struggling under the weight because they know that it makes them better. They never question their coach or blame him for their inability to lift heavy weights. They blame themselves. Not with judgment, but only with an understanding that they aren't there yet.

There is a famous book written by Fyodor Dostoevsky that really brings this idea to light. In Dostoevsky's book, there is a young Russian aristocrat by the name of Ivan. Ivan has a problem with God that he can't get past and looks at the bondage that people are born into along with the evil in the world around him. He says evil must be a byproduct of circumstance. There is no God for Ivan because he can't wrap his mind around a God who is all powerful and yet allows so much evil to go around in the world. Ivan decides, due to the circumstances of the world, either God doesn't exist or, if he does, he is evil. Since Ivan can't picture God as evil, he decides that there must not be a God.

Ivan is approached by his half brother, Smerdyakov, about the issue of God and evil. Ivan, who is wrapped in his own intellectualism, tells his brother that everything is permissible in the world but that he must decide what is beneficial for himself and society. He then tells his brother there is no God.

Smerdyakov takes this advice very literally and, in a rage, kills his father. When the crime is blamed on another of Ivan's brothers, Dmitri, Ivan decides that he must get to the bottom of who has done this deed. As he investigates, he ends up at the house of Smerdyakov. His half brother confesses to him that he committed the murder and says that Ivan was an accomplice.

Ivan is floored at the accusation of being an accomplice. He knows he never told his half brother to kill his father and can't believe what he is hearing. He demands an explanation as to why he is responsible for this awful deed. Smerdyakov tells Ivan that when he told him there was no God, he also said there was no right or wrong. If there wasn't right and wrong, then it shouldn't have mattered that he took the old man's life since Ivan and his brothers despised him.

It is in that moment that Ivan realizes why he is guilty. Ivan faces the reality of his philosophies and can no longer stand by them. Once he realizes his father has been killed, he knows that it is wrong even if he can't explain why there is a right and wrong. Ivan realizes that in his denial of evil, he has participated in evil.

As Ivan encounters his own guilt in his father's death as brilliantly depicted in *The Brother's Karamazov*, I also feel the shame of my participation in the disease of men. I can talk all day about passing the blame of my sin to a man in an ancient garden. But as I hurt the ones I love, and disdain the only one who truly loves me, I cannot escape the truth of the community where I belong.

I belong to the community of the fallen, the community of Adam. This is what the apostle means when he says we are in Adam. We are his followers and will follow where he has gone. Our sin leads to death, just as Adam's did. Adam brought death to all humanity when he chose to separate our race from God.

Adam is the old humanity. It is a people in bondage. A people bound to do the things that should not be done and reap the consequences of those decisions. The reason that Adam is the old humanity is because there is something new.

It's funny how something new can bring so much joy. As I am writing this, I am sitting on an American Airlines flight. We have been at a Ravi Zacharias conference, which was wonderful. If you don't know Ravi, you should. He and his wife Margie are two of the most exceptional people I have ever met. Ravi's apologetics bless so many people, yet it is the new things he brings to the field that provides so much joy to people.

Ravi brings compassion to apologetics. Though he is correct most of the time, he never makes you feel intimidated. At this early point in my career, I am no one special. A wonderful friend provided me an opportunity to have lunch with Ravi and Margie. Despite my youth and obscurity, they made me feel special. Witnessing the compassionate love of a conservative apologist is something most people never see. The experience brought me great joy.

On a slightly less serious note, I just had another experience that brought me joy. During a recent flight when the flight attendant asked for my drink order, I asked for a Fresca. I didn't think the order was strange, but apparently I am the first person to ever ask her for a Fresca in all her years of flying. She thought it was one of the funniest things she had heard in a while. I think part of the joke was that I am in my twenties and her, being an older woman, she hadn't had a Fresca since college.

I think the best place to start having a new perspective is while viewing our dreams. Often we think that our dreams are ours alone. We hold them tight and let them drive the hope of our lives. But is this what we should do?

What if our dreams were communal? What if we involved God and the people that we love in our dreams? What if we changed our thoughts from what we can accomplish to what God is already accomplishing in and through us?

When dreams die, we tend to blame someone else or even God. I know that this is exactly what I did with both football and when I had cancer for the first time. I felt that maybe God had given me cancer as either a punishment or to teach me a lesson. When we think this way, we are acting like Ivan from Dostoevsky's novel. But blaming God for bad things has consequences.

One of those consequences is that we lose our chance to grow. If I fail to realize that I am responsible for my own shortcomings, then I miss the reality check on one of the areas where I need to grow. The problem is that some bad things aren't our fault. Instead, we question why God would allow them to happen.

There aren't currently answers as to why things like cancer happen. The church says it is original sin. But that doesn't answer why certain things happen to certain people and others, who seem more deserving of punishment, never get sick. I can't answer why I got sick or why your love one died. I can only say that we have a choice in how we think about it. This choice is important: We can either say that God loves us and will help us grow through it, or we can instead, blame God.

I can't defend God, but I know I don't want to be Ivan. What are the consequences of me blaming God? What if people stop growing because they feel that they are victims of an uncaring God? Think of all the good things that would go undone due to being disengaged from the Kingdom of God! Think of all the growth you personally will miss

the good things that would go undone due to being disengaged from the Kingdom of God! Think of all the growth you personally will miss out on if you decide to be a victim. It robs you of an opportunity to be a more patient, loving, compassionate person with richer emotional character.

There is a fascinating story about a man who was a double agent spy who played both sides in a short war between the nations of Egypt and Syria against the state of Israel. The war began with surprise attacks by both Egypt and Syria that took place on Yom Kipper, the holiest day of the Jewish year. Though the war eventually ended in a stalemate, it drastically changed the political map of the Middle East because Egypt and Syria were able to take back control of the Suez Canal as well as other land that had been taken from them by Israel in the Six Day War.

What is most interesting about this war, is that at the center of it was a spy named Ashraf Marwan who was a twenty-six year old Egyptian soldier. What makes Ashraf Marwan such an interesting character is that, before the war began, he contacted the Israel intelligence agency and offered to give them his country's plans for the war.

Marwan struck an agreement with Israel that he would pass off Egyptian military secrets to them in exchange for $100,000 each time they met. Between 1969 and 1973, Marwan gave the Israelis information regarding the President of Egypt, records of the deals made with Russia for weapons and, most importantly, the detailed Egyptian war plans for recapturing the Peninsula of Sinai. Marwan even agreed to let them know when the surprise attack would take place.

However, if the Egyptians were asked who Ashraf Marwan was working for, they would have said without a doubt, that he was their man, through and through, not the Israeli's. The Egyptians have said that Marwan was part of their own plan for the recapture of the Sinai Peninsula. That it was because of his working with the Israeli army, that they were able to gather their troops at the Israeli border without suspicion. As they gathered their army for the impending attack, Israel heard nothing from Marwan and, as a result, didn't think that the soldiers massing at their border were any threat.

The desire of the Egyptians to recapture the Suez Canal and a large part of the Sinai Peninsula hinged on the ability of Marwan to deceive the Israeli military. While Israel waited for Marwan's word on when the attack would come, they ignored the information sent from observation posts at the border, therefore not making any decision until they had heard from Marwan.

When Marwan finally provided the information that Egypt was indeed about to strike, just twelve hours before the attack began, Israel was caught completely unprepared. Most of their soldiers had been sent home for Yom Kippur to be with their families. Marwan's information allowed the Israelis to mobilize their army and meet the attack of the Syrians on the Golan Heights and drive them back, saving the state of Israel. However, the attack from the Egyptians at the Suez Canal was a different story.

While Marwan told Israel that the attack from both Syria and Egypt would begin at 6:00 a.m. on Yom Kippur, only Syria attacked at that time. Egypt attacked four hours earlier. With the attack beginning earlier, the Israelis didn't have enough time to gather their forces to repel the attack and the Egyptians were able to break through their defenses. In doing so, they crossed the Suez Canal and took back most of the land they had previously lost.

According to the Egyptians, Marwan's deception was crucial in their ability to take back the Canal. Similarly, according to the Israelis, Marwan's information was likewise crucial in their ability to save the nation of Israel. Today, both nations, Egypt and Israel, celebrate Ashraf Marwan as their greatest spy. In fact, the Egyptian president Sadat awarded Marwan Egypt's highest medal, secretly after the war, for his contribution in the victory.

Marwan's role in the conflict of the Yom Kippur War remained a secret until several years ago when details of his actions came out in print. At the time, Marwan told those closest to him that he was becoming concerned for his own safety. In the summer of 2007, Marwan was found outside his fifth floor apartment where it appears he had been thrown from the balcony. He had been working on a memoir recounting his days as a double agent and they were missing from his apartment after he was found dead. All the recordings he had dictated were lost as well.

Egypt flew Marwan back to his home country where he was given a hero's burial. Thousands of people showed up to honor him, including some very high ranking members of the Egyptian intelligence establishment. However, he is still celebrated by the Israelis as the best spy the nation ever employed. They claim that he never betrayed them and, without his information, the nation of Israel would not be in existence today. The secret of who Marwan was really loyal to probably died with him and his stolen memoirs. While both enemies claim him as their own secret spy, no one is sure where his allegiance truly lay.

Sometimes we feel like God is Marwan. We aren't sure what side God is on. Our dreams die, and we can't figure out why God didn't help us. We may never know why God doesn't intervene to save our dreams, but we still have proof of whose side he is on. The life of Jesus Christ proves that God is on our side. We have to hold on to that one truth when our dreams die and we can't interpret God's activity in our life. God made a definitive statement about his loyalty in Christ and it says he loves us and is loyal to that love.

CHAPTER 7

What if?

Today is an interesting day. I am traveling to Minneapolis for a training session for my company. I am excited because I will be sitting down with the designers of a behavior assessment that looks at what drives people and how their strengths integrate best with other behaviors. Intellectually, it is a very stimulating subject and a great distraction from cancer.   The day is also interesting because I am getting to experience molting, which is what only cancer patients and birds experience. When I woke up this morning there was hair all over my pillow. I used a brush and there was hair in the sink. For someone who is vain, it is a rather traumatic experience even though there is nothing exceptional about a cancer patient losing their hair.

There is something exceptional about the day in that I am losing it. Yesterday I had a great afternoon with my pastor. He came over to the house and we talked about God for quite a while. The reason for the visit wasn't to discuss religion, but instead to engage photography, which is my pastor's other passion.

Pastor Glenn began practicing photography a few years back. I had no idea he was so accomplished. My wife Bailey heard that that he took pictures so, on a long shot, she called him. We had contacted many photographers hoping to get pictures taken this week because I was afraid that after my next Chemotherapy treatment I would be left with no hair and no pictures with my wife and daughter that didn't look like they were taken outside a concentration camp. I didn't want the only memories of my daughter and I to be pictures where I looked so different from who I am. I worry all the time about Ellie not knowing me. She hugs me and I know she loves me, but what does anyone really remember at age one?

Our pastor was a savior when it came to the issue of our pictures. He came over yesterday and took some great pictures of our family. We took both formal pictures and pictures of us playing with the cat. Glenn and I had a nice conversation when we were done. It was a great day.

Then today, I woke up, ran my hands through my hair only to find them looking more like a wookie than normal human hands. Not *all* of my hair fell out. I don't want to give you an overly dramatic account, but while I lost a lot of hair last night, I still have it falling on my computer keyboard as I write this.

It is another one of those instances where you have to ask if it is a coincidence or something more. I have stopped calling it a "God moment" because after thirty or more times the phrase seems overworked. But it is another proof that God is at work in my life. I can't explain it, but it comforts me. God is real. Real enough that he helps me get pictures taken the day before my hair starts to fall out!

What if there is more happening in our world than we can see? And what if there is more to the world to come than we can imagine? Before I got sick and was struggling with my faith, I had come to the conclusion that much of what I saw in my life as God's activity had nothing to do with God. To some extent, I believe this is true. When we attribute things to God, we must be very careful. Many times people blame things on God or attribute things to God that have nothing to do with anything heavenly. A great example of this is when people say everything in life is a miracle. No, I don't believe that is true. If all of life is a miracle then nothing is a miracle. A miracle by nature is a deviation from the natural law; something that couldn't happen according to physics, yet does happen.

The problem with counterfeit claims of God's intervention is that they lessen the impact of God's true appearances. It is static in the data. This happens all the time and we talk about it in children's stories. The "Boy Who Cried Wolf" is a great example, except, instead of crying wolf we cry "God." As I tell you about the moments I have with God, I want you to understand that I am not talking about miraculous intervention. Instead, I am talking about an unveiling of God's presence through the very unlikely and an honest assessment of feeling his presence.

If God will intervene in the issue of my hair, what might he do in all of our lives? Why does he do it in some cases and not others? This is an area that is gray for me. For two years I cried out to God for help and yet received no answers. I still don't have answers to my questions, but God has shown up. I don't know why he has and I know that he doesn't show up for everyone. The fact that he doesn't always show up this way has compelled me to tell my story so that they might provide comfort to others.

So what do we do next? How do we interact with God when we don't know if he will intervene? I believe a lot of people struggle with this question. I don't want to presume that I have the answer. These are questions I am dealing with as I face possible death while looking for the presence of the almighty entering my world.

I realize that God has already intervened for me in Jesus and that is enough to prove his love. Because I know God is real nor do I dispute the account of the apostles' witness of their experience with Jesus, I have a good foundation to build upon. This foundation is essential because it gives me the lens through which I view every experience of my life.

Building on that foundation, through the lens of God's goodness and intervention in Christ, I can say that none of the trials I face are placed upon me by a malicious or heartless God. If I can't blame God for the hard situations, what do I do? I take responsibility for what I can do, acknowledge what I cannot control, and trust that my life and and efforts are not in vain. I am not the victim nor is God the perpetrator.

Many Christians feel they are victims. They say things like, "It is not God's will that I get a job," or "The devil is causing me to be sick." These sayings are ridiculous and can become crutches for doing nothing. If you don't have a job, go out and find one. Network, improve yourself, and cold call until someone offers you work. If you have stage four lung cancer, it is not necessarily Satan. Millions of people get cancer and it has nothing to do with the devil.

What is dangerous about being a victim is that it takes the power from you. As soon as we start to focus on someone else doing something for us, we lose sight of what we can do. The truth is, we don't know if it is Satan or God, or a magical fairy that caused my cancer. It doesn't matter. This is a gray area where faith must shine through.

I have cancer, and it sucks! But here's the deal. I know God loves me because of Jesus, that heaven waits for me, and I can fight like hell because I don't have to worry about going to hell. Why I got cancer doesn't matter. If I need to know why, God will tell me. For now, Jesus is enough and the question I ask is, "How do I use the bad to make this world more like the Kingdom of God?" I ask this because the Kingdom of God is where all people will feel God's presence.

No matter the circumstance, we fight like hell to make this world more like the world that Jesus described. More like Heaven. The question is, what does God do and why should we pray? Before I began the publishing process for this book, it started out as a completely different book that was coauthored by a man named Paul Joslin.

I wish you could hear Paul's entire story, but here it is in a nutshell:

Paul's mom died of cancer when he was in college. When she was ill, many people prayed that his mom would live. Paul joined them in their prayers. Of course, he was broken when she died. He had so many questions and still does about why God didn't answer his prayer.

I have questions about why God didn't answer his prayer. His dad was in seminary and they were planning to become missionaries. They are God fearing people with great faith, yet God let her die. Some would say this is proof that prayer doesn't work. I believe they are right. If prayer is a mechanism to get what we want, then prayer didn't work for Paul. The question of why God let Paul's mom die, and the question if prayer works are two separate questions.

I don't know why God let Paul's mom die and I'm still a little mad about it even though I never met her. What if prayer isn't meant to get us what we want and instead is meant for something different?

What if prayer is a means of orienting our soul towards something that our mind doesn't easily perceive? What if meditation on the spiritual realm helps us to access more of who we are and more of who God is? Many people say that prayer is about having a relationship with God. The problem is that most would say God doesn't speak back. I would agree that many times he doesn't speak back, or at least I am unable to hear him. Therefore, how do you build a relationship with someone who doesn't speak back to you?

The apostles asked Jesus about prayer and he gave them an example. He told them to acknowledge that there was a God and that there was a heaven. He told them to acknowledge that he is good and he wants the earth to be a place like heaven. He instructed them to ask for help to get through the day and to forgive them so that they would forgive others. They were to ask to have help with temptation because God was all powerful and he wanted his will for humanity to be lived out on earth.

In another passage, Jesus says that God already knows what we need. There are also passages in the Bible that talk about getting whatever we want. If we are in line with God we can move mountains with our faith.

Prayer appears to be very confusing if you look at Scripture. I have banged my head against a wall trying to fit all the Scriptures together and make a nice neat package. Perhaps we shouldn't look at it that way. Instead of putting Jesus' words through scientific rigor, maybe we should look at the story as a whole and see where it leads us.

For example, at the end of Jesus' life he prays that he wouldn't have to die, yet God lets him die. This is in stark contrast to the passages where he raises people from the dead and says if you stay in line with God then you will get whatever you ask for.

If we look at the story of the Gospels, we see that prayer is important in linking us to God. It makes us aware of the reality that is beyond our physical perception. It can create miracles, but it can't be used to force miracles. It is something that shapes us and not God.

What if we ask the question about whether or not prayer works? Then we actually pray and look at ourselves to see if there is a change. Do we have the wisdom or knowledge to pray the right prayers? There are times when prayer makes things different. Like when Jesus raised Lazarus from the grave. It is another gray area as to why things happen with some prayers and not others. The area that isn't gray is that prayer brings thoughts to our conscious mind that change who we are.

CHAPTER 8

Does Jesus Change People?

Why do we see Christians do terrible things? How is it that people who claim to be changed often do worse things than people who reject Jesus? These are important questions that require answers. From the tragedy of the crusades to the terror of Civil War slavery in America, history is littered with examples of people doing terrible things in the name of God.

My first job at a large church was in Plano, Texas. Prior to that, I was teaching at a private Christian school but desperately missed preaching. As a result, I looked for any position where preaching would be a part of the job. A very large church was kind enough to take me on as an entry level minister.

I was going to work in what the church called Married Adult Three which meant working with adults forty-fifty-seven years of age. My supervisor was a man by the name of Joe Barron. I sat down with Joe to make sure it would be a good fit.

Joe was an older man who was very warm and personable. We talked for more than an hour as he shared his desire to help me develop my pastoral skills and his views about ministry. He conveyed a genuine desire to reach people for Jesus. I left the meeting encouraged. For some time I had desired a mentor and it seemed this man was going to be the one God provided.

The week before I was to start my new job, I received a call from one of my best friends who worked in the ministry and had served that church. Michael was really upset.

Michael was watching the news that day when Joe Barron's face appeared on CNN. Joe had been on Michael's ordination council so he immediately stopped to listen. With horror, he listened to the newscaster tell how Joe had been arrested.

Joe lived a secret life deeply entangled in sin when he wasn't at church. He was arrested in College Station, Texas for attempting to have sex with a thirteen year old girl. What Joe didn't know was that instead of a 13 year old girl, he was actually talking to undercover police.

When Michael told me that story, I will never forget the uncertainty that clouded my soul. The story made me want to cry, as it still does today. I wanted to cry for his family and for Joe. I also wanted to cry for a world where this happens, but there weren't any tears left.

Mostly I felt uncertain about God and life. I didn't understand why God let this happen. Nor did I understand what it meant for me. I had made a huge decision by quitting my job and was stepping out in faith, trusting that God would provide me with a new job. My new job turned out to be under a pedophile who was arrested before I could even train.

Rather than walk away, I went ahead and took the job. There, I worked in the same division with all the people who were betrayed by this minister. My first job was to clean up the contact list in my division. The contact list was somewhere around three hundred names of people who needed to hear from a minister. They ranged from people who just joined the church and needed to be welcomed, to people begging for a call from a minister because their spouse just cheated on them.

As I began to call the people, I realized some of the contacts were over a year old. There were people who had loved ones dying and families in danger who asked for a call a year ago but no one had called. The minister of the division had lied to his supervisor about contacting these people saying he called them all, yet didn't enter the notes into the computer. His supervisor unfortunately believed this man wouldn't lie and let it slide. The minister had lied and, as I picked up the phone, I was to deal with the consequences of his sin.

I can't describe all those conversations, only to say that they broke my heart. People were hurt and could not understand how a "man of God" could betray them. They were struggling with the question, "Does Jesus change people?"

If we are going to answer this question, we have to understand how the Bible says people were changed. The Bible makes sin very clear, and says no matter who we are or where we come from, sin is always fighting for control in our lives.

The idea that Christians are no longer living under the rule of sin and death is hard for many to grasp. You don't have to look to examples as big as Joe Barren to see that there are many professing Christians who still sin.

The idea of a Christian who still struggles with sin has been a problem for as long as Christianity has existed. In the early days of our faith, people would wait to be baptized until they were on their death bed so that they might live a life without sin after their conversion.

This idea may see ridiculous to many Protestants since we believe that salvation has more to do with the state of our heart than an observance of an ordinance. But the question was as real then as it is now. How are we to view Christians who sin?

The most amazing thing about our faith is that we don't deserve it. It has never been about our ability to be who we should be. There is a sense within biblical theology that a person is different when they accept Christ and that is where things seem a little gray when it comes to pastors and others who have done things for God and then become apparent "traitors" to the faith. Was Joe Barron really a Christian when he was engaged in the seduction of a 13 year old girl?

I can't answer that question. Instead, I can say that he wasn't acting in accordance with the commands of Christ. Christ says in John 14 that those who love him will obey his commands. However, Paul says in Romans that we aren't under the law but under grace.

Grace is the unmerited favor of God. The fact that we don't deserve it is really hard for people to understand. It is so easy to justify some sins while condemning Joe for his. The problem is that the cross is for the grace-covered traitor, whether that traitor is Joe or me. Therefore, I have to leave the question of heaven to God. I don't know if Joe repented or how that even works. I only know that the grace of Christ is unrelenting.

A lot of times Christians tend to act as if sin is our master. It is as if we have no choice but to sin and be stuck in it. Paul says this isn't the case. After we are brought from death to life, we have a choice. He tells us to not present ourselves as servants of sin, but instead to come before God and offer our bodies as servants for righteousness. He is trying to show the Romans they have been given freedom from the rule of sin. Why then, would they still serve it?

Think about it this way: If a slave lived during the time of the Civil War and was freed from his cruel, abusive master, would he ever go back? Then why would we go back to the cruel, abusive master of sin once we have been freed from it? We were once in bondage and slavery to sin, but no longer. We must stop serving our former master!

It is confusing to think that we serve two masters. The imagery Paul employs is hard for the modern mind to absorb. One writer described what Paul is trying to tell in a beautiful way. Imagine that you are a German who has never set foot in Japan. An opportunity comes your way to listen to an ambassador from Japan who describes his beautiful country and the amazing life of its citizens. As you hear the man speak, something stirs in you and you realize that more than anything, you want to be Japanese.

Overnight you are transported to Japan. However, upon your arrival, you find yourself struggling to be Japanese. You have the assurance from the government that you are a full citizen, but you don't speak the language and find yourself struggling to speak with people. You truly are a citizen, because the government has decreed it so, but you aren't able to act like a Japanese man. You don't know the customs and cannot speak the language, but one day you will. On some days you do things more like a German than a Japanese, but those days don't negate your citizenship.

I realize that this analogy doesn't answer all of our questions and is far from perfect, but it does help us understand the status of a grace-covered traitor. The traitor acts more like the sinner than the saved, but we don't know for sure what country he belongs to because that is an issue between the man and the ruler of heaven.

We are freed to follow God because of the Holy Spirit. But we don't always follow God when we have the Holy Spirit. One might wonder, then, "We are freed from slavery, only to be put back into slavery?" It seems kind of messed up. But the answer is yes. While we are free from sin, that freedom allows us to be slaves to God and his righteousness. It is a completely different kind of slavery. It is slavery to righteousness, not slavery of oppression and desolation. It means we are locked into GRACE!

For a Christ follower, there is certainty that no matter what struggles are encountered when walking as Christ walked, they are linked to grace through Jesus. This means that we can stop obsessing over our sin and feel the freedom of grace. Knowing you are loved in spite of what you have done or do, allows you to grow. The problem is that many people don't believe they are or can be forgiven. They don't embrace the Gospel and instead believe they are chained to the punishment of sin. Because of this, psychologically, they are altered and the possibility for transformation is limited. Remember, whatever you focus on expands. Focus on grace and grace expands, focus on guilt and something ugly expands.

I recently read a story about a man named Rom Houben. Rom was in the news because he had emerged from a vegetative state that he had been in for twenty-three years after a car crash. The doctors thought Rom had sunk into a coma, and later diagnosed that he had passed from a coma into a vegetative state.

Apparently, the difference between coma and a vegetative state is that in a coma the patient is unconscious and his eyes remain closed. It is as if he or she were asleep. In a vegetative state, however, the patient's eyes are open but he or she remains unconscious, and unable to think, reason, respond or do anything of purpose. The bizarre thing about Rom's story is that during the twenty-three years he was in a vegetative state, he was conscious the whole time.

Rom's parents refused to believe he was in an unconscious state for all those years and searched for doctors who would help figure out if he was unaware of the world around him. Finally, doctors were able to discover that he was conscious after a PET Scan showed brain activity of someone who was conscious. They immediately began trying to establish some form of communication. After so many years crying out for help without being heard, Rom Houben was finally able to communicate with the outside world.

Just imagine lying in a hospital bed after living through a serious car crash. You hear what the doctors are saying to your family never being able to live a normal life again. That they will never hear your voice again nor be able to see any sign of recognition. You are not supposed to be able to hear their words or communicate back with them. But as he says this, you are hearing what he's saying. You know you're conscious and that what the doctors are telling them is untrue.

You are gripped with fear realizing you're trapped inside your own body and no one may ever realize you're still there. Everything within you is screaming out to be heard. You scream out with everything you've got, but no sound comes. Your heart beats faster with anxiety realizing you may be stuck in a bed the rest of your life with no one around you knowing what you are thinking. Instead, you are trapped inside your own head, and your frustrated cries ricochet from one side of your mind to the other while never escaping your lips.

The prospect of screaming out with no one hearing would have to be an excruciating experience. Doctors said when they were able to help Rom communicate with a computer device, he showed a lot of anger and frustration. But thankfully, our cries for help do not go unheard. We do not have to shout and cry out for years and years without any hope that one day someone somewhere might hear us. While trapped, God heard our cries and longings for freedom from sin and answered them.

God sent his son, Jesus, to be our savior and free us from sin. Through the miracle of his death and resurrection, he conquered death and sin, bringing us freedom. He takes away the bondage of sin and death. What's more, he asks us to be his people and allows us to serve him to make this world more like heaven.

It's a little gray, isn't it? A little gray, and yet clear as day. All we can do is treat the people around us the way Christ has treated us by forgiving them. When people ask us why they should believe in the claims of Christianity, with men like Joe in the leadership, tell them men like him are the reason they should believe. If God forgives Joe, you should feel pretty good about your chances.

The sin that plagues us as Christians isn't our biggest obstacle to overcome. Instead, it is the biggest billboard for what Christ has overcome. We don't advertise that billboard because we want to - we do it when we have to. Let's use our God-given freedom well. Say a prayer for Joe today, shed a tear, say a prayer for me, and thank God that there is the opportunity for freedom. Freedom for a traitor, love for the betrayer; what kind of God do we serve?

A good one!

CHAPTER 9

The Dirty Kid

The church is filled with confused people pretending to understand. As humans, we like to pretend. From the time we are old enough to talk until the day we die, we love to "fake it until we make it." You see it in the little girl who says she can read but, as she flips through the pictures of a book, you can see she has only memorized what has been read to her over and over again. In the grown man who has never been a father before, you can see it in how he gingerly picks up his newborn child hoping not to drop the baby. You can also see it in the middle-aged woman, who wears teenage clothing that have been cut more than a Christmas turkey, trying to pretend she is younger than her years. We love to pretend.

In church, pretending comes as we say amen to the preacher, but we say "Oh crap" in our heart. There are so many people who act like they have it together but inside they are struggling with sin. As ministers we are not exempt from this pretension. Ministers are some of the worst pretenders in the church. How many times have you heard a sermon without an ounce of uncertainty and wonder how the minister could be so steadfast? It is not one sermon of certainty that makes the minister a pretender, it is a lifetime of sermons without questions that show him as disingenuous.

Are there certainly questions that cause us to ask God what he is doing? I don't speak here of questions about Christ's divinity or of his salvation. Instead, these are questions of God's action, or lack of action, in the world. These are real questions that leave us in a quandary. Questions like:

"Why did you let tsunamis destroy Thailand?"

"Why did you let the Holocaust happen?"

There are some that try to answer these questions with a simple line about evil or the natural order. I don't discount some of the validity in these answers. However, I do doubt the validity of giving these answers without the addendum, "I am not sure why." There are some things that we can't explain, but there are others that we can shine light on.

The question that causes our pretense is, "Why have you not taken this sin from me?" This is the question that causes men and women to act as if they are okay when they aren't. For the American Christian, most have sat in pews for decades and the thought that they still struggle with sin would surely cause them great embarrassment in front of friends and those in the church.

To avoid embarrassment, we run to religion. We have sin that we still struggle with every day, yet we come to church every time the doors are open. We are covered in guilt, but we numb it by forcing ourselves up at the crack of dawn to memorize Scripture. The problem is, the more Scripture we memorize, the more we realize how wrong our actions are and how guilty we are. What do we do in response to our guilt? We either go to church more or don't go at all. The apostle Paul speaks of this struggle in Romans 7:21-25:

> *²¹So I find this law at work: When I want to do good, evil is right there with me. ²²For in my inner being I delight in God's law; ²³but I see another law at work in the members of my body, waging war against the law of my mind and making me a prisoner of the law of sin at work within my members. ²⁴What a wretched man I am! Who will rescue me from this body of death? ²⁵Thanks be to God—through Jesus Christ our Lord!*

So then, I myself in my mind, am a slave to God's law, but in the sinful nature, a slave to the law of sin.

How is it that I can know Jesus yet I do these things? Have you felt lost in this question? Do you feel like the people in your church are either liars or are better Christians than you, since you never hear them say that they struggle with the same sin over and over again? Maybe your sin is "serious" and all you hear others talk about is their struggle to break free of jealousy or pride.

Many of us have heard the answer to this question. We tell them to "Find the will." Find the will to read your Bible or find the will not to struggle with temptation. We also find the will to memorize more Scripture and you will find the will not to struggle with sin. These are religious answers that often sound pious. When they don't work, there often are great consequences.

I have a friend who once told me the thing that frustrated him about Christians more than anything else was how inwardly focused they seem. While my friend was not a Christian, as we sat and talked I realized how right he was about how Christians often act. He said most of the Christians he knew were more concerned with being a "good moral person" than they were about helping out their fellow man. Most Christians he encountered were more concerned with trying to not to use off-color language, avoid looking at pornography, or not gossiping than they were about feeding the homeless or helping others with real needs.

Their own personal piety seemed to trump any need to serve others. In essence, Christians were great lovers of themselves but cared little for the world around them.

I have to admit, what he said really hit home. Even though he told me that I was different from the other Christians he had encountered, in my heart I realized I spent most of my life and energy as a Christian just trying to get by without sinning. Many of my days were spent concerned with meaningless attempts to read my Bible, and hoping not to fall into temptation. I thought being a "good Christian" meant rarely cussing at school and not partying on the weekends.

My daily focus was on myself and trying to find the will to live a "good Christian life" without sin. I wasn't focused on helping others find freedom, or loving them the way Christ did. Whenever I screwed up, the weight of the guilt of measuring up to "good Christian morals" broke me down to the point where I never thought I did anything right. My Christianity kept me from feeling like I was deserving of the "name" Christian. I struggled to find the will to stop sinning and, as a result, felt like God was scowling down at me.

Our churches are filled with people who are trapped in the slavery of guilt based on coming up short as Christians. What is our answer to this problem? Is it right that so many see the cross of Christ as an obligation to "find the will?"

For many years I thought that my holiness would be determined by my discipline. After all, we teach our young people that a "quiet time" is the key to personal holiness. If we were just more disciplined to seek God, we would be freed of our sin. This sounds much like how the Pharisees acted.

The Pharisees were a group of people during Jesus' time that believed the Kingdom of God would come if his people observed the law. If the people were disciplined and faithful, then God would see this and bring forth the messiah. Somewhere in the Pharisees' thoughts, it became more important for people to follow all the rules they set up rather than trust that God would bless them and change the world. Jesus' main issue with the Pharisees was that, in their pursuit of the rules, the people were lost in the balance.

In pursuit of perfection, the Pharisees pretended that their world was different and gave up trying to really help others. Love was given up in exchange for control!

If this is you, it is time to stop. Stop trying to be perfect and realize that you are loved and you are to love others. That's it. It seems a lot more gray and complicated than that, but when it comes down to it, you need to love God and love others. Once you realize that God loves you and you don't have to manipulate him, everything changes.

As I write this, I am on my way back from a training conference where I had an interesting conversation with a lady at my table. My hair was rapidly falling, so I had my head shaved during the first day of the conference. When I came in, this particular lady asked about my hair. After I told her about my cancer, she apologized for her bluntness and shared a story with me.

Her aunt was diagnosed with lung cancer when she was very young. She ended up living to the age of seventy-eight, which was awesome. The most encouraging thing about the story was a saying the aunt had. She would say, "Cancer makes you forget about the socks on the floor." Her point was that when you are faced with death, the little things are brought into perspective. I am facing death and struggling through my faith. From my perspective of dying within the next year, the most important thing in my life now is love.

My question to you is, "Do you have religious socks on the floor?" Religious socks are evil's attempt to use the small things to keep you from the big things. When you are forgiven, you are loved. Can you love and forgive? Can you stop worrying about your socks?

You can't make yourself perfect by isolating yourself in religion. A quiet time doesn't bring you to Jesus. The words "quiet time" don't even appear in the Bible. Jesus does spend time alone with God and shows us why that it is important. However, that is not all he does, nor is that what he is calling us to do.

Jesus told us to pray in the first person plural. It is remarkable that we are not taught this in our spiritual development. At least I wasn't taught this. I have grown up in western society where individualism is held up as the 11th commandment.

The hardest part about having real relationships is that they are messy. Getting close to people is hard because we all have the same problem; we do the things we don't want to do and the things we do are the things we don't want to do.

The Bible gives us the formula for allowing God to cleanse us. It tells us we will be cleaner if we go play with the dirty kids. I never wanted to be the dirty kid. Instead, I was the obsessive kid that went through all of 3rd grade with his hair so gelled that it moved the comb instead of the comb moving it. It goes completely against my nature to want to play with the dirty kid, but if I want my nature changed, that is exactly where I will find it.

Right now I am the dirty kid. Recently, my wife tried to book a massage but they almost refused due to me being a cancer patient. If you sit down with me, you have to be okay with the emotional weight of the reminders of death each time you look at me. You also have to deal with the awkwardness of not knowing what to say.

As the emotionally dirty kid, I have a lot to give you. You don't need to be scared to enter the emotion with me. There is great growth in that dirty, gray place of sitting in a room with someone who might die.

Most of us stop at this point even if we realize the truth of needing real community. We may intellectually know that we should walk through life loving our fellow man. But rarely are we moved to actually participate in that community.

When I was younger, there was a boy in my church whose father came down with lung cancer. It was awful. This strong man was overcome by the disease and was lost within a couple of months.

I will never forget his funeral and how I looked at his son and felt hurt for him. We didn't really hang out together prior to this time in his life. He was hyperactive and his behavior was hard for me to handle. He has since grown into a wonderful man, but when he was young he was a handful.

I went up to the young man after the funeral and told him how sorry I was. I told him that if he ever wanted to hang out that I would be there for him. I instinctively knew that he needed community in that moment and genuinely wanted to help. The problem came when the young man came over to my house and wanted to take me up on my offer. I am ashamed to say that I never spent any real time with him. Though I wanted him to know how sad I was for him, I wasn't willing to shoulder the burden with him. When I think back to that time, I am disgraced by my lack of action. My heart was true in the moment, but lacked the fortitude to enter a real relationship.

Are you struggling with making any progress in becoming the person God wants you to be? How about the evil that lingers at your doorstep? Maybe it is time that you take a more community-oriented approach. Who are the people in your life that you could walk with? We need people of all ages and backgrounds to surround us in life. Some need to be able to run as fast as we can. These are the people who have the same intensity for Jesus as us. We also need some whom we can set the pace with. These are people who are wanting to run, but are a little behind us in their abilities. We also need people whom we can help pick us up off the ground. And lastly, we need people who either don't know Jesus yet or are exploring the idea of getting to know Jesus.

Who are these people in your life? Maybe it's time to get a little dirty with them. It's time to love the dirty kid, because you're God's dirty kid and he loves you!

CHAPTER 10

What is God's Will?

What is God's will for our lives? This is a question that we all ask and one that can be very confusing. People take this in all different directions. I have even heard young people break off relationships because they said it was God's will. Others struggle with accomplishing things because they said that God didn't tell them to do anything different. Conversely, I have heard of people who accomplished great things because they said it was God's will. Historically (and eve still today), people have killed others and even declared war thinking it was the will of God. With all these different examples swirling around our heads, we must ask what God's will is for our lives.

God's will has been something I've questioned all my life. Why is it that I have stage four cancer again? Why did I get sick right after I left vocational ministry? Weird timing, isn't it? I left the church at the end of December, and by February I was in the hospital with pneumonia caused by a tumor no one knew was there.

Is God at work in this? Is he trying to tell me something? If so, how would I know what it is? This is an example of questions people have asked for forever.

Was it God's will for me to go back and play football and write a book? This question can have light through what the apostle Paul wrote in Romans 8:28-30.

> [28]*And we know that God causes all things to work together for good to those who love God, to those who are called according to His purpose.*
>
> [29]*For those whom He foreknew, He also predestined (preordained) to become conformed to the image of His Son, so that He would be the firstborn among many brethren;*
>
> [30]*and these whom He predestined (preordained), He also called; and these whom He called, He also justified; and these whom He justified, He also glorified.*[4]

These verses are some of the most read in the entire Bible. They are popular because of the sense of apparent security they provide. In times of need, people seek to be comforted. I have heard Romans 8:28 quoted over and over again as a comfort to those that are hurting or dealing with grief.

In my own life, this verse was quoted when I was sick with cancer. I am not sure how many times I saw the letters or had it spoken to me in the form of a prayer. I even memorized the verse trying to find comfort in the words of our Lord even as I struggled over its meaning.

Many see the words of the apostle Paul as God controlling every aspect of our lives. In many Bible translations, and without a thorough

---

[4] Rom. 8:28-30 ESV

understanding of the letter's context, it can seem as though God has heartlessly determined we are to suffer. When the words are quoted by a person outside of our suffering, they can often seem trite and condescending. However, when quoted by God there is only one understanding.

Christ suffered to make right our suffering. Some would look at Christ and his death and say that there are many throughout history who have died in much crueler ways. Many people who've taken this position are not belittling the suffering of Christ but are instead deeply moved by the immense tragedy of our world. They are the people touched by the horror of Auschwitz or robbed by the terror of a serial killer. I cannot say that I understand the depths of suffering in the world, nor do I know the horrors of the cross. What I do know is that he who knew no evil experienced the evils of the gates of hell so that those who believe can experience eternal life.

It is that discrepancy in experience that helps me understand that God's statement in Romans 8:28 is not without compassion because Christ has been where I never have to go. When he says that the things of this life can be used for good, I believe that he understands our pain.

If we are in Christ, God uses the hardships of our life for a specific purpose. This is very different than God causing human suffering. The verses are not commenting on the origin of the hardships of life, although Paul touches on this in the previous chapter. Instead, these verses give us the way to live and the way to see life.

Paul says that God causes all things to work together for good. This is a very difficult phrase for those who have suffered. The husband who has lost his wife, the daughter who has lost her mother and the parent who has lost a young child may have a hard time seeing the good in the passage.

One of the most important phrases in this section of Scripture is found in the phrase, "For those who are called." "Called" is a reference to those who have found the truth of the Gospel. They are freed by grace.

Why has God allowed us to continue to walk in a gray world filled with evil lurking behind every corner? God's purpose is seen in the process he has preordained. You will notice that I have placed the word *preordained* next to the word predestined in the translation of Romans 8:28.[5] The reason for this is our association with the word destiny. We see too much determinism in these verses along with evil.

The process God has preordained is the one that moves us toward the image of his Son. Christ died, but he did not die in the normal way. Jesus did not have his life taken from him, he gave his life. Jesus was the suffering servant who endured the hardship of this world so that those who saw his sacrifice might give up the pursuit of self. It is in the surrender of self that we find ourselves birthed anew and the beginnings of a movement to become more like our savior.

God's will for our lives is that we become more like Jesus. He has called us to enter the process of surrender and to endure suffering that we might trust him in every aspect of who we are and what we love. Our struggle is whether or not we fully trust God. Do we trust him so that our lives can be lived differently?

We find that the greatest trust is required when the world is dark and the reasons seem gray. If we are able to explain every detail and see the greater picture with clarity, then we aren't required to trust the one that leads us. If we know the bigger picture, it requires a deep trust to walk through the pain of a dark world where the details are gray.

Pain and evil are the darkness of the world we live in. We have seen a great light, but our ability to see the world around us remains hazy and our understanding of the places we step on the path we walk is limited.

I have a prognosis that says I will die in eight months. My daughter won't even remember me because she will only be two and a half years old. At this stage in her development she is barely old enough to speak. Today I got home from a trip and I went upstairs just so I could watch

---

[5] Wright, The New Interpreter's Bible, 601-602.

her sleep. Tomorrow I have to leave early to go to the hospital and I won't see her again until the evening. I have been gone from her for a week and it feels like my heart has been ripped out. What if I only have eight months to live? What if she doesn't ever get to know her daddy who loves her so much?

It scares me to ask the question, "What is God's will for my life?" Was it his will for me to fail in football? Was it his will that I get sick? Those are questions that no one can never answer for me, yet I ponder. While I speculate about the details and watch some confirmed and others dissolved, I know what has been ordained for me.

I am one of the called. Just as God called Israel out of the wilderness, he calls me and all who have been touched by the Gospel out of the darkness. Those of us he has called are led to a life of surrender and sacrifice. He has called me to trust even when I don't understand the immediate.

Here is gray faith. One day I will see my daughter again. But will I love God less if he takes away all the years I want with her? Will I still love him if I miss her wedding and the birth of her first child? Surely I would like to live to hold both of my girls. However, if my death means that others have a better glimpse of God, then I will say as Christ said: "Not my will, but your will."

I am not giving up. No, instead I'm acknowledging the gray nature of faith. I know I will live again, yet I don't know when I will die. Can I trust what is at stake? I don't know if I could have if God had not shown up in my life in such a strong way.

Do you trust God enough that you would allow him to take the best parts of your life so that others might know him better? I may be scared as hell when the time comes for me to die, but I am fighting so that my death makes known a little more of heaven. Standing in front of the first, like Shadrach, and say, "He is good and he is God, whether he saves me or not." I also say, "My wife and my child are yours, God, and I trust that you will take care of them when I can't."

There is so much that I don't know, yet I say, "I love you God!" I don't understand how I'm able to say it, but am so thankful that I am able to. I don't understand the whole story about how I got to this place, but I want to share some of it so that maybe you will be able to stand and say, "I love God," even if I don't know what is going to happen.

This is God's will for our lives. We love God and, in turn, love others no matter the circumstances of life on earth. All other details merely fade away.

CHAPTER 11

Why I Still Believe

Have you ever tried to order flowers in London? For some, this would seem like a monumental task, but for the current generation this really shouldn't be a hard thing to do. You simply go to proflowers.com, pick your bouquet, and enter your address for delivery. (Consider this a royal tip for your next anniversary, guys.)

The first summer my wife Bailey and I spent apart, I found out that ordering flowers in London was not as easy as I thought it would be. I was in Waco, Texas going crazy because I hadn't seen Bailey for months. She told me that I could only call her every other day, which I hated. I seriously thought about buying a plane ticket and flying to London. But when I got onto the travel website Orbitz and saw how much plane tickets cost, I rethought my approach.

With the price of a plane ticket lurking in my mind, I went to the love bullpen of every American male. The flower shop. There, I found a beautiful bouquet of lilies and began to submit my order. It was only then that I realized I didn't have the address for Bailey's dorm.

No address, no problem. I jumped on the phone and called the college Bailey was attending. In the 21st century, a little pond the size of the Atlantic is no real separation. I knew the English, like Americans, spoke English. Since I spoke English, it would only take a minute to ask the person working the front desk at the college for the address and Bailey would have flowers in no time.

What I soon realized was that they may speak English in England, but it's not like speaking English in Texas. After calling the front desk four times, and pretending to have different accents each time so that the guy answering wouldn't realize it was me again, I still had no idea what the address was for Bailey's dorm.

When I finally realized that the person on the other end might as well be speaking Chinese, I understood that there was much more separating Bailey and I than a small jump over the pond.

For me, one of my greatest fears is being alone and separated from the ones I love. These days I am scared about being separated from the people I love. Inside I know that it won't be for long because I have a feeling, a longing deep inside of me, that heaven is going to be awesome. I believe I will get to explore new worlds, have conversations with wonderful people, grow as a person, worship God through all kinds of activities, create art, and do other awesome things.

Why do I believe this so strongly? In this book I have explored a lot of questions. But some that still have me wondering are:

* In the Old Testament, why does the Bible seem to condone the killing of infants?
* What is the plan of salvation for the world when so many people never hear the name of Christ?
* How does Satan exist if God is all knowing and all powerful?

* Why is it that God lets us pray about taking away the same sin for years without interceding?

* If so many babies never pass the zygote stage of development, what happens to them?

* Why would God make it so hard for us to identify exactly who he is?

* On what authority did the council 300 years after Christ have in coming up with the most complicated decision on who Christ was and in determining people's faith based on their belief in that complicated idea?

* How is it fair that Joe Barron might go to heaven, yet a teenager who dies in Asia and has only heard the Gospel one time might not get there?

And, why do I have terminal cancer?

I could go on for hours with all these questions and get even more technical. However, I think you get the point, since many of you may have some of the same concerns. I almost left the faith because of these questions and many others. But then God showed up. I still don't know why he did. After going through depression for two years and feeling abandoned, all of a sudden he pops up everywhere

The first place I saw him was shortly after my cancer diagnosis. After getting the news, I became very depressed. Shortly thereafter, we got into financial trouble and had to move. Then I took a job with Regency Nursing and Rehabilitation Centers, the company where my dad works. The price of housing in the Victoria area was so high, due to a huge oil and gas development, that we decided to stay with my parents.

It is embarrassing to be a somewhat successful twenty-nine year-old man with a family and be living with your parents, but that turned into a God moment. My dad was able to track the progress of my cough and give me multiple medicines. We had exhausted our options when one night one of my lungs pretty much stopped working.

I was upstairs with my wife watching television when my left side started to shoot with sharp pain. I began coughing and wheezing. I couldn't stop coughing and the pain in my chest was different than it had been before. My dad ran upstairs and gave me drugs and breathing treatments. The next day I received a CT Scan and x-rays. They found the tumor because of that CT Scan. Normally, according to the pulmonologist, a patient walking in off the street would only get an x-ray. With only an x-ray they would have assumed it was adult onset asthma because of the pneumonia I had earlier in the year. I don't know if living with my dad saved my life, but it definitely gave me a better chance of living.

The other thing that happened due to living with my parents was that my wife and baby have grown close to them. Before moving in together, Bailey and my parents weren't that close. They had never spent a lot of time together, but over the last six months, my wife and mom have become good friends and my parents have gotten so much time with their grandbaby!

In college my wife was a cheerleader. My mom, on the other hand, was a microbiology nerd. They are not two people one would think would hang out together. Now Bay goes shopping with my mom and cooks meals with her. I can't tell you what a comfort it is to know that my wife and daughter are bonded to my parents. I don't want Ellie to forget who I am. I want her to know her daddy and I am so much like my parents that she will for sure know me if she knows my family. The bond that has been created because of this situation lets me know that Ellie will know me.

For me to end up staying with my parents wasn't just a onetime incident. It took me having a mental and spiritual breakdown at my ministry job. It took us having financial problems because of a hospital visit and a real estate economy that wasn't at its greatest. It took me turning down a position in Corpus Christi because I was having a physical breakdown from pneumonia and, in turn, a mental and emotional breakdown. All of these things cullieded to let me end up in the house with my parents and eventually let me find my way into the perfect role at Regency!

When I went to get my first CT Scan, I didn't notice it, but one of my former elementary teachers was in the waiting room. Though she thought it was me, it had been a long time since she had seen me so she didn't say anything. Even weirder, she had a dream about me playing football in high school the night before. Seeing me that day at the hospital, she felt that something important was about to happen to me. Shortly after, she found out about my diagnosis through Facebook and broke down into tears.

My first grade teacher's daughter contacted me and wanted me to know about her story. She said that she believed that God had something special for me in all of this and described her mother's dream. It was very overwhelming for someone to contact me this early in the process with something so spiritual. Looking back at it now so many months later, I can only say that some of what she described in the dream definitely happened to or for me. She talked some about an illumination or a glow in the dream and I can tell you that I have been illuminated and have seen God in ways that I never expected. I don't know what her dream meant, but at least that part is very real for me and the fact that she dreamt about me the night before I found out I had a tumor is very strange.

Shortly after this, there was a Friday and I had to write a five-thousand-dollar check that we lacked the funds to cover. I wrote it and hoped for the best. The next day I was on the golf course. We were on the ninth hole and it had been a weird round.

The round started when Dad and I were about to tee off. The first hole is always nerve racking because there is no driving range to practice on in Cuero and your first shot could go anywhere - including oncoming traffic. I was a little perturbed when this guy decided to stop his run and stare at us as we teed off. I didn't really need extra pressure - Dad and I aren't exactly Tiger and Rory.

We actually hit the ball off the tee okay, which was the first blessing. The next blessing came when the man came over to talk to us. He was a good looking guy in his forties, maybe. He looked familiar, but I didn't know him. He said hello and then asked if I was Mr. Heard. This threw me a little, but I said yes and my dad came over. He explained that he didn't know us but that he had been following my story and that he had prayed for an opportunity to pray with me. What was strange was that he wasn't usually off work at this time, but something had happened and he got off early and came for a run. When he saw me, he knew that it was God and so he stopped. The man then proceeded to say a prayer so beautiful that it brought my father to tears. We walked down the first fairway at the golf course overwhelmed by God's goodness and the grace of a stranger.

We were on the ninth hole when my cell phone rang. It was Cody Wallace calling to ask if he could provide some help. Cody is two years younger than me and was my center in my senior year of high school football. He went on to play for Texas A&M and then a number of professional football teams. At the beginning of the year, he prayed that if he got picked up by another professional football team he would give money to people needing help. He picked another couple and me to receive money. Within days, five thousand dollars was in the mail!

You believe in coincidences and so do I, but I wrote a check for $5,000 and Cody calls and says that he prayed and he is sending me $5,000? We hadn't talked in years, at least not more than a handshake after TAMU crushed Baylor.

The night before I found out I had lung cancer, I decided to write about my condition. I was feeling very drugged, but I got on my old blog (www.andrewbheard.com) and wrote a post. That post saw 55,000 views in the last four weeks. More recently, my blog saw 20,000 views in two days. I got a call from a billboard company who felt moved by my blog. They decided to give me billboard space all over the state for free!

The day I found out I had lung cancer was a really hard day, especially when I told my family about it. By the afternoon I was especially feeling down. I realized that I had moved so much, and done such a poor job of keeping up with people, that there was nobody I could call to talk about what was happening to me. I wandered around the house and found myself looking out at the backyard. I felt terrible, and the worst part was that the aloneness I felt was my own doing. Within an hour one of my best friends, who lives in China, called to talk! It had been over a year since we had spoken and he picked that day to call. Jon Spear was a messenger from God that day.

I walked around my backyard and got to tell him that I just found out I had lung cancer. He was the perfect person to talk to and I hadn't arranged it at all. All I had done was send him a LinkedIn message a month earlier giving him my new contact information. Jon is one of those guys who I won't talk to for a year and it is like we talked yesterday. He is one of a couple people who is like a brother to me.

I felt so alone and Jon made me feel like not only did I have friends, but I had a God who was watching out for me as well! I got off the phone and walked into the house a little steadier and ready to minister to my family.

As I got into my treatment, there are only so many things one can do to stay active on Chemo. I decided to play golf as a means of exercise. One day I was out on the course listening to an audiobook. On the fifth hole I looked over and saw a man fall out of his golf cart. I didn't know if what I was seeing was real or if they were joking around, but it was an older group of men and I knew some of them, so I doubted it was a practical joke. I ran over to see if he was okay and saw that he was grabbing his chest. Immediately, I called 911, but I also realized that we were on the golf course and they might have a hard time finding us. I jumped back in my cart and left the man in the hands of his friends. I drove to the club house to try and find aspirin. I thought he might be having a heart attack and aspirin seemed like the right thing to do, but finding aspirin was a lot harder than I thought. After realizing that I wasn't going to get aspirin before the ambulance, I headed to the street and waited to drive the ambulance out to the man on the course. The ambulance showed up and we escorted it to the fallen man. The man ended up in the ICU with broken ribs and a number of other conditions, but he is okay now and even came to a sermon that I preached here in Cuero.

I don't think I saved his life that day. I think that his friends would have taken care of him, but it is interesting that I was there and able to help. We have a friendship and bond now and I didn't even know the gentleman before. He came to a church that he had never been to before to hear me speak and that meant a lot to me as well.

One of the other regulars at the golf course was my neighbor Don, who was a very nice man. He was the one who took me out to play golf when I was sick with cancer at age eighteen. I really loved Don and his wife Norma. A couple of weeks after I got sick, Don found out that he had the same cancer as me. He died four days later. What is really strange is, the last time I had cancer, my neighbor at the time also found out he had lung cancer. He died before my treatment was finished.

I don't know why Don died or why my other neighbor died. I do know that it is really weird that both happened and that my wife is here for Don's wife Norma and that Norma is here for Bailey. Did God arrange that? I have no idea. It is a gray area that I can't answer with certainty. But do you see how all these gray shades start to form a pattern?

Recently I lost my hair. I knew it would happen, but was hoping it would hold out for a while. We got nervous before my second treatment because we realized we didn't have any family pictures with Ellie. We called several photographers and couldn't find anyone who could accommodate us. Then we heard that my pastor had become a photographer. He was kind enough to come over on a Sunday and take our pictures. We got great pictures and it was a good day, well worth remembering. The very next day I woke up to find hair all over my pillow.

Did you catch that? *The very next day*, a large chunk of my hair fell out. I'm not talking two weeks later or randomly here and there over the next month. A big chunk fell out the next day! I am not saying all of my hair fell out the next day, but enough that it meant a lot to me that my pictures with my daughter were done before it happened.

There are more examples that happen every day. I can't explain it other than to say that God has appeared in my life. It has provided a deep sense of his presence - something I haven't felt in a long time. I know that God loves me. Though I don't have all the answers, I do have God's love.

The reason that I believe, despite all my questions, is even if I can't prove God exists, I have felt him in my life. I cried out like Job and God showed up. He didn't show up in the way I thought he would, and I have no idea what is going to happen, but that is okay. God loves me (just like he loves you) and his love is changing my life.

I believe God is trying to communicate with me that even if we don't have all the answers, he is there for me. There are questions that none of us can answer. We need to accept this and be more understanding of others that don't understand or who disagree with us. It is important to show grace and love to all. There are a lot of gray areas in our faith. We have to acknowledge them with transparency and honesty if we are ever going to grow.

God is real! He is intervening in my life and I believe he also does in the lives of others. I don't know if he will save me in this life, but I am positive he will save me in the next.

You have that same assurance. Now what you are going to do with it? The world needs people who know God loves them and there is more than this life to look forward to. The world needs his people because together we have the power to change the world.

Our faith is not black and white, it is full of gray things that we don't have the answer to. But we have "that one thing." We know that God loves us, which is enough to make heaven in our world even if the circumstances of life are hell. May we be faithful through the gray patches so that the world sees the light of God's love as it illuminates the path of our lives, wherever it may lead

CHAPTER 12

Walking in Uncertainty

So I wasn't really walking, I was lying down. Truthfully there wasn't much walk left in me. I had just had a Chemo treatment and the back of my mother's car was about as far as I was going. My mom drives a Chevrolet Malibu, which is a good car, and has a descent backseat to sleep in.

There is an Academy off of highway 59 in Houston and Mom had gone in to pick up a few things. I was dazing in an out of consciousness. I would rather be flat asleep, but sometimes that isn't an option. The ring from my cell phone pulled me from sleep. I looked at it and didn't have the number programed in. Recently my cell phone had been through a lot so that didn't surprise me. While I didn't know the number, it was a Houston number, so I decided to pick it up.

I wasn't expecting anything from the hospital. It had been a long time since I had any test done, but when I answered the phone, it was my Oncologist's Nurse Practitioner. She is a very sweet, lady and when I heard who it was, I still had my guard down. She asked me how I was feeling and went through some short pleasantries. Then came the pauses.

Let me explain pauses to you if you are not familiar with them. As a speaker, they are powerful tools. They let the audience know that something is coming and if you are really good, the audience isn't necessarily sure if it is something they should like or something they should fear. In case you were wondering, pauses from your oncology department are not good.

"Andrew, we got the results of your brain MRI." Awkward pause. "Let me get Dr. Heymach to talk to you about them." Oh, the next thirty seconds of bliss/terror. Brain, scan, and cancer are all words that should be banned from sequence in the English tongue. People always talk about how time will be different in heaven, but they don't really understand it. A day is like a thousand years and so on. We'll have those three words strung together for you and wait and you will know exactly what is meant by the relativity of time.

My doctor is very good. He is very smart and smart enough to deliver bad news in the best way. He told me that I had tumors in my brain, my cancer spread, but we had a plan and we were going to try our best to save me. It wasn't the news we wanted, but we would face it head on.

I choked back a tear and told him thank you. I told him thank you for the way he spoke to me and the kind of doctor he was. I really meant it. I had recently sat with a radiation oncologist that told me I was going to die and there was nothing he could do about it. Well forget you, doc! You might not know what to do, and I sure don't, but that doesn't mean I'm giving up or that I have to die. Needless to say that other doctor and I are parting ways. I will have more to say about that later.

The phone conversation ended quickly and I was left in the car waiting on mom. I cried. I cried a lot. Having lung cancer spread to your brain is never a good thing, even if you are more optimistic than that crappy, bedside mannered, radiation oncologist.

I knew that the likelihood of my living had gone down significantly from a medical standpoint. Dr. Heymach's office told me I had two significant tumors, one the size of a golf ball in my cerebellum. I shouldn't really be able to walk, but I was walking, and giving sermons. The size of the tumor and the rate of growth meant that I could die within weeks - not month or years, - weeks!

The idea of losing everything so quickly overwhelmed me. The problem was, I didn't know what was going to happen - no one knew. I could die in a few weeks, or a few years, or tomorrow, and no one could tell me when. The uncertainty of that situation clawed at my soul.

My mom got in the car and I told her what had happened. She was quiet and just listened to me talk. It was really smart and really kind! We cried together and talked about family. It was a hard ride home. I called Bay and her family and let them know. They needed to know that I might die soon, but it was a terrible conversation to have.

Bailey and I never thought about my cancer spreading to my brain. I am not sure why, but it was something that we just hadn't processed. The brain is a scary place, because it controls who we are and there is so much about the brain that we don't know or understand. Maybe uncertainty, and the fear that it brings, kept us from thinking about the scenario of cancer in my brain.

There is a Scripture passage that many people misunderstand, where a man misses what is really going on because of fear. In Luke, after the centurion's servant is healed, John the Baptist's disciples come to Jesus and they have a simple question. John's disciples want to know if Jesus is the one or if they should expect another.

The strange part of John's question is that John baptized Jesus and affirmed his role in the Kingdom of God. John played such an important part in the beginning of Jesus' ministry, and now he questions whether or not Jesus is sent from God? Why would John do this? Why would someone who has seen and said so much now go back on his faith? The question of faith comes up in the Bible on many strange occasions and we find ourselves asking, "How can they question God? They just saw him do such and such!"

Here's the thing. John is in prison! He is about to die and Jesus isn't going to save him. John has been preaching that the righteous and the unrighteous will be sifted, but John is about to be killed and Jesus isn't going to help him. As John sits in prison for doing what is right, namely calling out a ruler for stealing his brother's wife, he wonders if Jesus is the bringer of the Kingdom of God where there is justice. If Jesus is bringing justice, why is he going to die? This doesn't seem right! The unrighteous are going to live and John, who has done God's will is going to die.

The small cell must have pressed in hard on John as he knew he was about to lose his head. He sits there and wonders, *God what are you doing?* Filled with uncertainty, John reaches out through his disciples to Jesus and all Jesus does is tell him not to lose faith. Jesus leaves his friend, his cousin, and the man whom he calls one of the greatest men to ever live to sit in the uncertainty of death!

I know a little something about how John the Baptist feels, and it sucks! Each day I wake up and I don't know if I am going to die. I know people are praying for me like crazy, but that doesn't mean that I will live. I know that I would like to do things for the Kingdom of God, but that doesn't mean I am going to live. I have to sit in the uncertainty of not know what God's plan is and trust him.

The hardest part about trusting God is my wife and daughter. My wife and I have fought a lot recently because I am so obsessed with trying to make sure their life is taken care of when I die. The truth is, I can't take care of them and force their lives to be perfect. They will have to walk the road that lies ahead with or without me and I have to trust that God will walk there with them.

The problem is, I know that God leaves you in the prison sometimes, and I don't want that for my daughter. I don't want her to sit and wonder if she will be saved or if she will be left and beheaded. The other real problem is that I don't want to give up the illusion of control! If I am alive, I feel like I can help control how things go for the ones that I love.

I know the truth is that I can control hardly anything. I can only control my reactions to the things that happen. I can control myself, that is enough, but it never feels like enough. I want my wife and daughter to be happy. Is that so bad?

It is not bad, but I have found that it is not healthy. We must grow in our faith. We must grow in our uncertainty. Growing in faith is not a matter of being so assured of God that we get what we want. Many people think this. They think that people of great faith are so close to God that they pray and then they get what they want, but this isn't how it worked for John the Baptist and it isn't even how it worked for Jesus.

Growing in our faith is hard because it means we become very small. As I trust God, I realize that I am not as important as I thought I was, and yet I am more loved than I knew that I was. When faith is small, the person is big. When I trust God less, I must trust myself more. This is where things get very tricky.

Some people believe that God controls everything and that we are so small that we must just say, "This is God's will," and accept whatever is put before them. The problem with this perspective is that it is wrong and arrogant. When we say things like this, we assume that we know the will of God. This is a dangerous assumption! God is too big, too smart, and too holy for me to understand his will completely. I may get a glimpse, but even with that glimpse I must be careful with what I think I know.

Growing in faith is the ability to say, "I have a glimpse. I have encountered God and now I will walk forward without complete knowledge in the trust of God's character as it has been revealed to me through Jesus and life." In this walk, I humbly accept that I don't have the answers, but I take action anyway.

I look to see what good I can do and I do it! If I mess up, I ask for forgiveness and reevaluate my perspective. Having faith means the comfort of knowing that if we mess up, there is a way to reconcile our transgressions. This is the great comfort of faith, but there is little comfort for the man who see what could be done and does nothing because he says it is not God's will. There is no faith in blaming God whether it is for evil or good left undone.

When we found out I had brain tumors, we cried, but we didn't give up. We decided to have brain surgery and there is no promise that it will work. They are going to drill four holes in my head and I am scared out of my mind - literally. I know that my chances of living have gone down scientifically, but my God hasn't changed. I don't know if Jesus will come and save me or if he will take my head, but either way, I know that he heals. As I sit in the uncertainty of whether he will heal me or not, I know that my faith is growing, even if it is a bit gray.

CHAPTER 13

Locked In

It took weeks after finding out that I had tumors in my brain before we could have anything done about it. Things at really big hospitals don't work at hyper drive. The other problem with really big hospitals is that they work on a lot of procedures and sometimes the person gets lost in the number.

We were sitting in a sterile room waiting for one of my doctors. The side effects from my treatment had been much stronger than they were supposed to have been. We knew that a lot of that had to do with the brain tumors that we had just found, but after talking to my brain radiation oncologist we were somewhat optimistic that things could be contained.

It was a stab to the heart when my other doctor came in to talk to me. He was flat in his tone and not warm, not particularly cold, just not warm. It was the way you felt about an elevator painting. It is there and it doesn't really look bad, but it really wasn't going to move you one way or another.

The doctor talked about my radiation treatment that he had administered. He had given me a month's worth of radiation to my main mass in my chest and two high dose shots to my arm and my leg. I had seen the reports he sent to my father, one of my attending physicians, and I knew that he only gave me the radiation to the other spots because Heymach and I demanded it. It annoyed me that he wasn't really on my side, but it didn't really matter as long as he helped. It was when I learned that he didn't help that I got infuriated.

"I didn't irradiate the spot on your pelvis," the doctor said, then just looked at me. "It is outside of protocol and it doesn't matter what I do, you are going to die." I just stared at him. I didn't yell, I just kind of bobbed my headed and looked at him. It was like he was a hotel fish tank. I could hear what he was saying and I wanted to punch him in the face, but I just bobbed like I was watching one of those bloated hotel fish.

I shook his hand and said okay, but damn it, I wanted to punch him in the face. We had a long discussion about treating all my metastasis before we started radiation and he agreed and then when it was over, he just decides to tell me that he doesn't feel like treating one and will leave that cancer in my body for now! Are you kidding me? I have a two year old! There are words that still go through my head that I coulnd't bring myself to type, but I'm sure you can conjure up a few on your own.

I still can't believe he did that to me. Looking at me like I am a hotel painting for sale with marker number 474031 as the bid number. I might not be Jesus or Michael Jordan, but I'm a whole lot more than 474031. Anybody is more than some dumb number attached to a file. I don't care if I have a 3% chance of winning! I once hit three homeruns in one game and I would have hit a fourth if the centerfielder wouldn't have made such a great catch at the wall. I took a football team to the state finals when I didn't weigh 150 pounds, as a sophomore, and the same year I jumped 23' in the long jump, and I'm WHITE! I'd like to take that 3% chance and kick you in the groin with it!

Sorry. That was not my westernized-Christian moment (I get one every ten pages or so). I love Jesus, but I'm not a saint. I need you to see who I am. It is important to me. I'm not just a number or an author, I'm the guy that lives down the street from you and it is important that you don't forget that. It's just that, being me is what makes this story special. It's not really about me, it's about something more. Something that I want you to have.

What I don't want you to be is locked in! That is where I found my-self when it was finally time to do my brain surgery. I had tried to prep myself the best that I could and I thought I had done well, but I was wrong. The morning came and they wheeled me into a room. I knew what they were going to do, so I asked for drugs. Sometimes you need drugs - trust me!

They gave me the drugs and then they locked my head to a chair and the sweet nurse with the New England accent held my hand and told me it would be okay. They drilled four holes in my head and locked a "halo" around my skull. The halo and hole where going to be used for measurement purposes. They took me to an MRI machine where I had tests done and was taken to a waiting bed. It took a couple of hours for anyone to come and talk to me, which I thought was weird, but I was drugged, so it didn't seem as weird as it did to my dad.

My brain radiation specialist is a sweet lady, and she came into the room and delivered the worst news in the best way. She told me that there was a problem. I didn't just have three or four tumors - I had twelve!

Twelve tumors in your brain is not what you want to hear. My fam-ily started to cry. My doctor quickly explained that we had to make a decision. It was against protocol to Gama knife a brain with that many tumors, but she was willing to do it for me if we gave the approval right then. My other choice was whole brain radiation which could leave me severely impaired. She gave us the options and stepped outside.

We all looked to my dad. "If she is willing to try, I say we let her do it." I agreed with his assessment and started eight hours of brain surgery.

I did okay for most of the day. You have to realize they didn't put me to sleep for this. It was laser surgery and I was in a tube suspended by four nails drilled into my head which were locked into a framework to keep me from moving. Most of these surgeries only lasted three to four hours, which would have been great!

The problem was that mine lasted twice that and by the end, my pain medicine was no longer working. I didn't feel good, to say the least and didn't know how I was going to make it through the last twenty minute session. When the session started, I started the Jesus' prayer, "Jesus Christ, Son of God, have mercy on me, I am a sinner." This is a prayer from Teresa of Avila and it works in breathing movements. You breathe in Jesus Christ, you proclaim Son of God by breathing out, you breathe in his mercy, and you breathe out your confession of sin.

Breathing and prayer have helped get me through a lot of things, but it didn't get me through this. I asked how much longer and they told me eight minutes. It was the longest eight minutes of my life! I tried to breathe and pray and I made it to two minutes left before I told them they had to get me out immediately!

Immediately didn't really happen. There was some kind of distraction in the hall. My head was locked into a frame work of nails that kept it facing straight up in the air on my back and I could feel the vomit rising. I couldn't stop it. I tried to fight it back. I fought as hard as I could with sheer panic. I might die choking to death on my own vomit. There was no way I was entering heaven with that story, but despite my efforts, the vomit came.

I puked and bile flew up in the air above my face. I tried to close it off so that it wouldn't go back down my air pipe. I could feel the nurses reaching and screaming from me as they pulled me out of the tube. The finally got me up and I puked again all over myself and the sweet nurse who had cared for me all day. It was a terrible feeling!

I was shaking and ashamed. I was a grown man covered in my own vomit and I had been very afraid of dying in my own vomit. You would think with all that I have gone through, dying while throwing up would scare me, but it sounded about as bad a death as one could have.

I sat on the examination table not knowing what to think. I was terrified that they were going to put me back in that tube. The women began to cut my clothes off of me, which was a relief from the terrible smell. I almost cried when I heard the doctor come in and tell me that I didn't have to go back in the tube. They had given me enough radiation already and I was free.

How is it that faith and freedom work together? Jesus says that he came to set us free, but he also calls us to action and to be different. This is a stumbling block to many people. There are many people who feel that being free would require a Jesus with no obligations or restrictions. They feel like they might suffocate if they are locked in to what Christ would have them do.

I will not pretend to be an expert on the law and grace. It is too complicated a matter for a mind struck with so much medicine and riddled with tumors. I can tell you that grace means being locked into nothing but the knowledge of the goodness of God! This is faith.

Faith is saying, I know not what is to come exactly, but I know the character of the one who will eventually bring it to an end. This is frightening because it means that we are locked in and have to deal with the good or terrible that might come our way. We may not be able to move our heads, save our child, or rid ourselves of a disease, and yet we must trust.

It sounds stupid. Trust when it doesn't make sense? Trust when you can't see the outcome? This is where the academic, agnostic would pity me and at times I have pitied myself. The thing is, life is more human than that abstract pondering.

You have met someone who says they will save you. They don't say how they will save you exactly or what they are up to. You don't know everything about them, but you are closer to them than anyone you have encountered before. They leave and you begin to look for your friend. You don't see him exactly, but you see weird things that remind you of him. You try and live like he did and your life is better. You also call out to him for help, but he doesn't come back and directly help.

You are left with the knowledge of what he did and how great your friend was, but the question of, can you trust him to come through on his end of the agreement? Here I find myself locked in! What Jesus, my friend, brings me is so much better than anything that I can do. I get mad at him because I don't know what's going on and I can't move my head to the side to see what's happening, much less move my head so I don't throw up on myself.

Christ asks me to hold my head still while he shoots lasers into my soul and tries to fix me. He asks me to hold my head still while the nails hurts so bad I vomit. He asks me to trust him even if I die in this life and he wants to know if I will do it. I cry as I write these words because my answer is, YES! "Yes, Jesus I will do it even though it hurts like hell and I am so scared I will miss my baby girl and my wife!"

I'm locked into to you and it is not because you make sense! I am locked into you because you don't make any sense and you show up anyway. You are like my wife! You drive me crazy. I don't understand you, but I love you. You can't seem to communicate anything that makes good sense to me, but somehow I know you are more right than I am.

Many of you have no idea what I am talking about. You have so many questions about religion. Join the club! I have all those questions too! A bunch of them don't make any sense, no matter what Christian apologists tell you.

Here is my suggestion to you: Forget the questions and find the man. Find Jesus and you won't lose the questions, but they will change in significance. You can't sit with a man and say he is not there. If you experience God, then you can look at the questions from a different vantage point. You may not have the answers, but the world will be different.

The question is: "How do you find Jesus?" This is an answer I can't promise you, but I will tell you what I did and maybe that will help you on your journey.

CHAPTER 14

Finding God

Where do you start to look for God? There have been movies, books, and civilizations built around the idea of where or how to find God. It seems a funny question if it is in God that, "We live and move and breathe." There can be nothing outside of God or he would cease to be God, and yet he can feel so far away. Even switching the pronouns, makes us feel uncomfortable and out of place, yet God is beyond gender and in Jesus within gender.

So what do we do?

When I moved back to Cuero, Texas, I moved back in tears. I failed as a minister at a large church in Dallas. There is no other way to say it than that I failed. It doesn't matter why. It is what it is. I didn't fail everyone and it is not that I did nothing good, but I couldn't be their minister anymore and really, I didn't know if I could be a Christian.

I wanted God and I wanted to understand him, but as I came home to my parent's house, I have never felt as far from God as I did in those days. I felt abandoned in my questions and my search for God. I felt abandoned by God's people. I had a counselor ask me if I expected the church to help me find God and I told him, "Yes!" He seemed shocked by this, but I didn't understand why the church wouldn't be the exact place to find the answers I sought.

I don't even know that I wanted answers as much as I wanted to feel God's presence and not feel abandoned, but I got neither. In many ways, I got the opposite! I got screamed at and judged at the church. I wasn't a good enough minister to someone's kid or my theology wasn't right. I love getting judged on my theology by people who have no idea what they are talking about and spout heresy without knowing it about every five seconds. It is like getting kicked in the nuts by a five year old and having to smile while their parents watch and nod in agreement. Sorry, I know that is vivid, but it is true.

All that to say, I wasn't in the best place when I came home, and I had no idea how to get to a better place. The first thing I did was, I stopped going to church. Most pastors would say, "Bad idea!" but honestly, it helped me. Church wasn't a place where I felt God. In fact, I had so much resentment that church was more like hell for me. It was the place where I felt most pulled from God.

What was really interesting was the way I began to feel God at work. I took a job with Regency Nursing and Rehabilitation Centers. It is owned by a nice Jewish man and a former 7th Day Adventist Seminary Student turned accountant. Neither man practices religion the way I was used to, and both use words that I never heard in my previous job, but I found something in these men.

Both men were different than I was, but both men believed in me! It was very strange because I had no experience and they had no idea what they were going to do with me, but I was overwhelmed by their belief and acceptance. The whole company made me feel welcomed and believed in! It was really weird. They had no idea who I really was or what my skill sets really were. They just seemed to love on me in this secular corporate way.

The company's affection began to change me. I didn't give any sermons or really even talk about God much. I made friends with a great guy who was a Jehovah's Witness. At the time, he wasn't a very good practicing Jehovah's Witness, but he was a great guy, he still is and I love him a lot. His name is Andrew as well. He is the black Andrew on staff and although he is younger than I am, I really feel close to him.

None of these people at Regency judged me. Even when I made a really dumb comment to one of our Vice Presidents and had to apologize over email, she didn't judge me or hold it against me. I said I was sorry and didn't mean what I said the way it came off and she continued to treat me great! At church, she might not have talked to me for years! I felt bad for my comment for weeks because I knew, taken the wrong way, it would really hurt her feelings, but the fact that she let it go and assumed that I really didn't mean offense blessed me so much! I tear up thinking about that because it is something so small, but someone assuming the best about you and giving you forgiveness really lets you feel God! Janice did that for me! She let me feel God!

At work they finally found out that I could do something to help the company. I could speak. I have given a lot of sermons in my short time and there isn't a lot of difference between a good sermon and a good recruiting pitch. I believed in Regency because of what I had seen in my short time and that was all I needed to put a good talk together to get others to believe.

When you can take what you are good at, and you like doing, and have practiced for some time and apply it; things go well! Things went well with my recruiting and I felt more of the resentment and failure fade away. Success can heal psychological wounds and God was giving that to me in my new job. He also gave me a place to love people without it having to be forced.

At church, we have to love people and they know it. Well, you are supposed to love people and they know it. At Regency, I was free to love my bosses and coworkers just because. My boss told me I was an idiot in front of a bunch of people once, but I got to just love him after it and I did. It wasn't forced. I didn't have to swallow my pride. He insulted me, but I just didn't care, I just loved him.

One of my bosses is Heber. He is from Brazil and he is a competitive, hot-headed guy. He is a lot like me with more Latin flare. Another of my bosses is named Donovan and he is from a small town next to Cuero, Yoakum. They were our rival growing up, but it is basically the same kind of town I grew up in. He and Heber are amazing golfers and also very competitive. Both of these men are my father's age and I love them both. I can't tell you exactly why, but from the very first, I have felt this way about them. It is like God put me in this job and said, "Here are two men you can really like, and love."

My other boss is the owner of our company and his name is Don. Don has been there for me from the first time I had cancer. He got a ball autographed by Roger Staubach, my football hero, when I was sick the first time, and he didn't really even know me. He was the first one to interview me for my job at Regency and he was the first to believe in me and tell the company that they needed me. I think Jesus used a Jewish man from Dallas to start to heal my wounds and to bring me home so that I could be in a safe place to fight for my life! Interesting, isn't it?

I don't know how to find God. There isn't really a map, but I do know that having people that believe in you is a part of it. People are a big part of finding God. God is in people and when two lives touch, the Kingdom of God can be felt pushing through the lies of this life. This life will tell you that you aren't important and that things don't mean anything, but things always mean something to other people. When you realize that you mean something to other people, you can begin to feel God. Maybe it is because in the realization of your worth to others, you feel your worth to God... I don't know exactly, and this book isn't about me knowing.

I can tell you that my church, the place where God met me, was in a corporation that manages skilled nursing facilities. He met me without religious words and gave me a people to love. That is where the road started, but it did not end there. People were about to play a bigger role than I could have ever dreamed, and I still haven't quite woken up!

CHAPTER 15

God Sweeps In

I have been through the ringer when it comes to finding God. In the church, people talk about discipleship. A disciple is literally, "A disciplined follower of a master." What it means is becoming more like Jesus. The problem is, how does one accomplish such a task?

Most conservative Baptist churches will tell you that it starts with reading your Bible! They beat quiet times like a dead dog and give horrible guilt trips if you don't practice the discipline. The problem is that reading your Bible doesn't make you more like Jesus. It lets you know more of who Jesus was, which is very important. I have read the Bible over 10 times from cover to cover. I stopped counting so I can't give you an exact number, but I have been through the material a lot.

I can tell you with certainty that all that reading didn't make me Jesus. I also have prayed a lot. In undergraduate we would spend three hours every Thursday in silent prayer and each day we would meet for two hour quiet times of writing, reading, and prayer. I didn't graduate with an awesome beard or the ability to walk on water. Why is this?

You can't force God. You can't make Him work on your time and you can't beat yourself into becoming more like him. I am not saying that there was no good done from the time I spent in prayer, but it didn't solve all my problems or overwhelm me with the presence of God. I know that many teenagers and young adults turn from the faith because of this. They follow the pattern to finding God set out by the church and then they don't see reality change. It is a terrible feeling.

You either feel abandoned by God or unworthy. You question what you did wrong or why you would believe in God in the first place. If you put out so much effort and God does nothing, then why believe or try? This is exactly how I felt when I came home to Cuero after serving as a minister. I came to the end of my rope and said, "God if you are real, I need you, but I have nothing left to give." I said my piece and went quiet on the subject.

When I got sick with cancer, you read about how God began to appear in my life. I hadn't prayed, really prayed in over a year. Even while I was working at the church, I would say prayers but the deep place of meeting between me and God was shut down. I hadn't been to that place in so long and yet I watched as God moved me and things in my life to reveal himself. I don't know why he did it, but he did it on such a great scale that being thrown from my ship and swallowed by a whale was only a stone's throw away.

My insurance wasn't what I thought it was before I got sick. I thought that I had a high deductible plan that would cover any major issues and I would pay a large portion for all the small visits. What I found out was that I had a high deductible with a max cap of $50,000. The problem is that when you get stage four lung cancer, $50,000 doesn't really go that far. In less than six months, I exceeded my cap and owed over $30,000 in medical bills. This was money that my young family didn't have and the idea of dying and leaving them with no life insurance and medical bills just made me sick!

One of our sweet family members set up an online donation fund for us. It was a nice gesture, but I honestly never dreamed that it would help us reach our needs. I just assumed that we might get a few thousand dollars, which would be such a blessing. My dad is a doctor and I thought that no one would give to my young family because of my dad. I am crying because I was so wrong!

As I have been telling my story at www.andrewbheard.com I shared the link to our fundraiser and shared about our financial situation. The blog has been an amazing evidence of God in that it has seen over 120,000 people come through and read about God and my journey. Those kind people, some I don't know and have never met, have given us over $28,000. I would have told you that was impossible. It went from $1,000 in one day to a blog post and a couple days later $14,000. I really couldn't believe it.

It got even crazier than our online fund. A lady that doesn't even live in Cuero anymore heard about our situation and called a couple of the cheerleaders at the high school. That day they gathered about ten people and decided to do an event fundraiser for me and my family. Within a couple weeks there were 2,000 people from my small town of 7,000 wanting to help. I had no idea this was going on!

I heard that a group of people wanted to throw me a golf tournament and fundraiser and I was very thankful, but it turned into so much more. The day of the event blew me away and still does as I sit here. They sold over $15,000 worth of t-shirts before the event even started. There were thousands of people who showed up to participate. We had the largest 5K run that Cuero ever held. People, who had never run, ran for the first time for me! I couldn't believe it.

I got to get up on stage and say thank you and tell them about the power of our community and the great way they changed my life. I told them about God's love for them and that no matter where they were at that moment that they could move forward in life and be more of the person that they were meant to be.

There it is! It is about becoming more of the person we are meant to be and God is in the middle of making that happen. There are some things that you cannot force. God could not force me to love Cuero the way I do now. He couldn't make me see the greatness of his actions in these people. He had to let me see it.

God cannot force me to trust his nature. He has to let me feel it and see it at work. If I could control these things by forcing myself to pray, it wouldn't be relationship. I don't know what it would be… I guess religion. I hate the whole "it's a relationship not a religion" thing because church is a religion. However, life is not a religion. Life is a process. One we can allow God into, see him in, or shut our eyes to his presence.

What I love is how God has forced his way into my life through people. He has shown me his character through people. Not church people or holy people, just normal, loving people. Normal people who, in an extraordinary way, raise over $100,000 for a young family at a one day event in a town of only 7,000 people. How is that even possible? That was the question I asked Sheila and the Halls as I sat in the living room crying when they told me how much money they had raised. I still don't know how it is possible. They changed the lives of my wife and daughter in a single day! I was afraid for the future and now my girls have no debt and will havet the house paid off. I can't say thank you enough. I just cry when I try. I can't tell you what it means to feel the overflow of God's love through a community of people. It is the most amazing experience a person could ever have! I can literally feel God's love pouring out on me and it threatens to rip my heart open.

I don't know why he has done this for me. I don't know why he doesn't do it for everyone, but I know I have to tell you about it because it is so important. He loves you the same way, and there will be a day when your soul feels this way. I don't know when that will be. I suffered for years with depression and doubt and God didn't talk to me, but as he does now, the flood gates have been thrown back and my soul is awash in a torrent of love.

This is what happens when God sweeps in. He did so, on the cross in Jesus, and he has done so recently for me. You have to hold out and wait on him. Faith is waiting on him. It doesn't have to be perfect. You can get mad and cuss, do whatever, but hold out for him.

Finding God has a lot more to do with him finding you. It is not that he has to search you out - it is more like he is courting your soul. If you are one of those people who needs something to do, here is what I recommend: Practice love!

Of all the things that make us more like Jesus, none compare to love. Of all the things that have convinced me of my faith, none compare to love. When love reaches out from another person and touches you, it leaves a real spiritual mark. The human condition is one that is not meant to be alone. Babies die that aren't held when they are little. What do you think happens to your soul when it goes too long without being embraced by love? It shrivels and turns in on itself in the most unnatural way.

When God sweeps in and opens your heart with love, it is a painful process of realizing what you missed! You missed all that you could have been when you were feeling the power of another's love flowing into your heart. You missed all the joy of your love flowing into others' hearts. Then you realize all the love that you have been keeping God from pouring into your life and you break! If you can get to that place of breaking, then none of the arguments will matter! All the gray issues of religion will fade away. You will care about love. How did you love your mom? How well are you loving your wife? Is there someone that God has put in your life to love on? These are the heart of the questions that should consume our soul.

These are the true questions of the Gospel of Jesus Christ. The Gospel of Jesus Christ is concerned with the Kingdom of Heaven and you will never get closer than when you are loving God's people. The Kingdom of God is bigger than creed, confession, or knowledge. Before there were creeds, there was love. Before there were confessions of faith, there was love. And before the knowledge of the Trinity, there was love.

When these things pass away, there will be love. Creeds will be irrelevant, confessions will be irrelevant, and theological knowledge will be irrelevant when we walk with the one who is the reason for all these things.

I leave all this three steps behind me in the pursuit of growing in love. If my ability to love well is what will carry me furthest into eternity, then I should focus on that and let it be the lens through which I look at every other issue and, more importantly, every other person in my life.

Life on this earth is not over yet, although it may be soon. The rest of my time I walk in peace, in the quiet gray questions of our world, illuminate with a faith full of doubts, walking with a God who makes all the doubts pointless.

About the Author

The most interesting thing about Andrew B. Heard as the author of this book is that he is still fighting cancer and doesn't know if he will live. His diagnosis of stage 4 non-large cell lung cancer has no cure and few survivors.

Andrew is a survivor. In the year 2000, Andrew was a highly recruited high school athlete when he was diagnosed with stage four lymphoma. It took nine months, but Andrew beat that diagnosis! Immediately after beating his cancer, Andrew enrolled at Texas Tech to play football.

The spiritual experience of facing death changed football for Andrew and so after one year of football he quit football and graduated with a degree in Communication in two years to go to seminary. With his little sister, Rene, at Baylor University, Andrew decided to head to Baylor's Truett Seminary.

Andrew found Seminary to be a hard place spiritually. After one year, he broke down and thought about leaving, but a few hours of prayer later he decided to write his first book, "Your Best Life Later" and go play football again. Andrew showed up at the walk on tryout at Baylor and it went great. Two years later, he had met his beautiful wife Bailey, a cheerleader, written and published a book, lettered in football, and completed his 93 hour graduate degree in Divinity.

Andrew now has expanded his family with the addition of his beautiful daughter, Ellie. He has fought his cancer for 9 months when his prognosis was 8 months and spends his time sharing the God encounters he has had since his diagnosis. Andrew doesn't know how long he has on this earth, but his hope is to inspire as many people as possible to see the face of God.